BOY OF THE LAND
MAN OF THE LORD

BOY OF THE LAND MAN OF THE LORD

ELAINE CANNON

BOOKCRAFT
Salt Lake City, Utah

Library of Congress Catalog Card Number: 89-83391
ISBN 0-88494-722-X

First Printing, 1989

Printed in the United States of America

This is a story of a lively farm boy
who became a distinguished prophet of God—
a family man for whom the world became home.
This is the story of Ezra Taft Benson,
born on a farm and anointed in a temple,
whose commitment to Christ permeates
his own life of sacrifice in service
that ranges from a farm in Idaho
to the cabinet of the president
of the United States of America . . .
and to the inner sanctuary of the house of the Lord.

This is the story of a boy of the land, man of the Lord—
for in the seed of the farm boy was the prophet.

Contents

Acknowledgments

People need heroes, models, examples for their own lives and for teaching situations. This little book was prepared in response to many requests for a *select* gathering of incidents and influences that helped shape the person known and loved as President Ezra Taft Benson, prophet and President of The Church of Jesus Christ of Latter-day Saints.

A project of this nature has required the assistance of many, including the Benson family. I acknowledge the valuable resource of faithfully kept records; the inspiring personal moments recounted by devoted Saints whose paths have crossed with President Benson's; the appealing work of artist Robert Barrett; the expertise of the publishing staff at Bookcraft. I am grateful to all.

I need only add that it has been a pleasure to bask in the light of President Benson's balanced and directed life.

Introduction: A Prophet's Life

It was September 24, 1988. The television camera focused on President Ezra Taft Benson as he listened to his own message being read by President Thomas S. Monson to the sisters at the general women's meeting in the Salt Lake Tabernacle.

This was one of those occasions when watching the meeting on television rather than attending in person proved the greater blessing. The face of President Benson reflected the image of a certain kind of father—a loving patriarch, a caring shepherd, a loyal friend, and a man of the Lord whom a person could fully trust and follow in confidence.

Ezra Taft Benson, prophet and President of The Church of Jesus Christ of Latter-day Saints, is a spirited and spiritual man. This was evident in a remarkable way on this occasion, for in his face shone the yearning he felt for the good of the sisters of the Church. Clearly he was experiencing a fervent reaching of the heart, a yearning that his concerns for the personal growth and fulfillment of the women would come to pass. The camera picked up the love shining in his smile, the radiance coming from within him.

And for many of the women, watching him was to have their souls warmed and their hearts forever changed.

That single incident brought forth hundreds of letters from women viewers, who expressed their gratitude and feelings of peace that the prophet was indeed their champion. They were ready to follow. They were committed to following his example in scripture study and to preparing themselves for the role of Mormon women as particular nurturers, teachers, wives, and mothers.

On other occasions young Boy Scouts have flocked about the Grand Scouter, President Ezra Taft Benson, an indication that this kind of boy wants to be *that* kind of man some day.

So powerful is the personality of President Ezra Taft Benson that an ever-increasing number of men are striving to follow his example as head of a family, seeking to become the kind of father that justifies the term *patriarch*. President Benson's unique approach to family life—his intense concern for his posterity, his gratitude and reverence for his noble ancestors—is impressive and is the basis of this book. His methods are based on eternal principles as followed by a man of character. This has produced a close-knit family devoted to the gospel and to being disciples of Jesus Christ.

A key element in the life and teachings of Ezra Taft Benson has been his love for the Book of Mormon. As President of the Church he has taken the Church by the hand and led the membership into a diligent and purposeful reading of the Book of Mormon, which has changed lives and strengthened testimonies.

Ezra Taft Benson was born August 4, 1899, in Whitney, Idaho. He was called to be an Apostle on July 26, 1943, and was ordained to that office on October 7, 1943. He was ordained President of The Church of Jesus Christ of Latter-day Saints on November 10, 1985. Before the time of his becoming President of the Church, his professional and Church leadership experience had spanned more than a half-century.

Having obtained a graduate degree in his field of agricultural science and having nearly completed a doctorate, President Benson has had more formal education than any previous President of the Church. He is the only General Authority of the Church who has served in the cabinet of the president of the United States of America, and this while serving as an Apostle.

During his varied career he has distinguished himself repeatedly and served unflinchingly. He has been entertained by top political leaders, royalty, and celebrities of the major nations of the world. Yet he says that his greatest love always has been for God and His children, with a special love for his own ancestors and descendants. Moreover, he experiences great joy in moving within the circles of the priesthood, doing the work of God.

He married Flora Amussen on September 10, 1926, and they are the parents of six children—Reed, Mark, Barbara, Beverly, Bonnie, and Flora Beth—and have numerous grandchildren and great-grandchildren.

This book is a collection of incidents in the life of Ezra Taft Benson that reveal the qualities and characteristics of a God-inspired boy who became a true latter-day prophet of God.

1

A Boy of the Land

Nobody knows what a boy is worth,
We'll have to wait and see,
But every man in a noble place
A boy once used to be.
                    —Author unidentified

There is a farm in Idaho set apart from all the other farms that lie on the slopes and basin floor of a spectacular valley on the Utah-Idaho border. This farm is the birthplace of Ezra Taft Benson, a prophet of our day.

A mountain range near that farm rises nearly ten thousand feet, adding majesty to the valley that holds the farm. The river early trappers and settlers called the Bear runs through the valley and is said to be the largest one in the western hemisphere that never reaches an ocean. It wanders a five-hundred-mile route (ninety miles as the crow flies) through three states before coming to its lower end in Cache Valley. There, interestingly enough, it increases considerably in volume from the flow of several mountain streamlets.

The land is nourished by the river, and pasture grasses are plentiful. The soil is rich. The years have taught the farmers that they really don't have to plow before planting—they just work the soil, but not as deeply as a plow would. At least that's the way it was in his youth, according to Ezra Taft Benson, hero of this story.

Cattle thrive in the valley. Gardens mushroom. People of character likewise flourish in this environment. The Bensons were people of character, and here young Ezra Taft waxed strong in body, heart, and drive, and grew in obedience to and love of God. After years of preparatory experiences he became the thirteenth President of The Church of Jesus Christ of Latter-day Saints.

Born August 4, 1899, in Whitney, Idaho, Ezra Taft Benson was the first and tallest of eleven children. He grew to be broad of brow and shoulder, with lively eyes and full, smiling lips. He was athletic, quick to learn, and willing to work. His belief in truth was a firm focus at each level of his life.

From the beginning it was noted that Ezra Taft was unique. It was said of him, as the prophet Samuel said of David of old, "The Lord hath sought him a man after his own heart" (1 Samuel 13:14). This child grew, and in all the aspects of his life served the Lord with all his heart, might, mind, and strength.

At the time Sarah Dunkley Benson, wife of George T. Benson, Jr., was expecting her first baby, two other Benson descendants in the valley were also with child. One day the three women—Lulu Parkinson, Louise Alder, and Sarah Benson—arranged to make a trip to the Logan Temple to receive prenatal blessings, after the tradition of the times. Traveling by horse and buggy allowed for a good deal of visiting among these relatives. Each was hoping for a boy. Lulu and Louise already had two girls each. Sarah was eager to begin her and her husband's new family with a baby boy.

But there was another reason why they all wanted sons. The first boy to be born of one of these three women would be the oldest great-grandson of their distinguished family patriarch, who was the first Ezra Taft Benson, an Apostle of God and one of the original pioneers. He was a captain of ten in the first party to enter Salt Lake Valley with Brigham Young in July 1847.

All three had boys when the time came, but Sarah's was born first, and he was given the name Ezra Taft Benson. Later he was presented with a scabbard and blade as well as a cane that belonged to the first Ezra Taft, his great-grandfather, who had owned them as a soldier in the Nauvoo Legion. His name was inscribed on the blade.

It was this first Ezra Taft Benson who was sent by Brigham Young to strengthen the settlements in Cache Valley. It was he who established the traditions of maintaining strong family ties; of having a family going generations deep who would build, cultivate, colonize, and replenish the earth; and of serving as an instrument to refresh the souls of men through powerful teaching of the principles of God. This Ezra Taft Benson was a living example of what he taught, and that example became an ideal for his great-grandson, Ezra Taft, to follow and became an integral part of his life's fiber.

Years after he had left the farm where he was born and reared—after he had become a nationally known figure of respect and importance—Ezra Taft Benson returned as a featured speaker in the community of his birth. On that occasion he shared his feelings about the place and the people instrumental in shaping his life.

"I grew up here. Here those lasting impressions of youth were implanted deep within me.

"Here I had the advantages and blessings of the atmosphere, example, and inspiration of an ideal Latter-day Saint home—of which there are no better homes—a home where I first learned to know God and His wonders, a home where we had simple but implicit faith that God truly answers humble prayers and gives guidance to those who seek him.

"Here I first saw in my family, neighbors, and associates the finest characteristics of mankind: inward peace, faith, humility, integrity, charity, courage, thrift, cooperation—and the value of good hard work—all ingredients of sterling character.

"Here in this valley I first learned the virtues and graces so well exemplified by the Mormon pioneers. Here I learned to work—with my hands, with my head, and with my heart. Here on a typical Cache Valley farm I learned that great lesson—the value of work."

Looking back to his beginnings now, Ezra Taft Benson says of the farm in Idaho, "This is my beloved home." He'll point to a group of farm buildings and describe each, its beginnings and its use. "We used to have 'Benson Brothers Farm' painted right on the roof of that old barn. We all were born and reared here. This is where it all began."

The house on that farm in Idaho started out as two rooms. It was built by industrious people who had a long view. Ezra's father, George Taft Benson, Jr., got the timber out of the canyon. He built the house almost entirely himself. Ezra's mother, Sarah, made all the linen and the carpets for the floor. She put straw under the carpets for comfort and warmth.

The day George and Sarah Benson were married was the day they moved into their new house. It was completely furnished and paid for, and they had done it together almost without any other help.

George bought forty acres from his own father, whose property bordered his own. Later he bought forty more, and finally he had one hundred twenty acres stretching in an L-shape. This was their farm in Idaho, and the family operated it until some years after the father's death.

Ezra Taft Benson remembers those days as important preparation for all of his life's mission.

"I drove a team when I was four years old, and not many years after this I was riding horses to herd cattle. I learned early to milk cows; we had seventeen holsteins. This became, and remained, a major responsibility during my growing years—this and digging potatoes and sugar beets, shucking grain, putting up hay, and doing all the other chores that fell to the oldest boy on a farm."

An old mill still stands in Whitney. It was there that young Ezra, in a wagon and team, used to take the family's grist to be processed. It was a water mill, and Ezra liked to watch the workings while the miller would grind the Benson family's wheat into flour. Sometimes they would simply trade the wheat poundage for flour already milled. But either way, going to the mill and back with a team of horses and a load of wheat or sugar beets proved an ever-fresh adventure. It was a time of learning for a curious young mind as well.

President Benson recalled an important lesson from those days. He wrote:

"When I was sixteen, a neighbor gave me a job of thinning a full acre of beets. This was considered a large day's work even for an experienced adult farmhand; it was back-breaking, done in a bent-over position, using a wide-bladed hoe on a handle about eight inches long. I started at sunup. When the sun went down that night, I was dead tired, but the full acre was thinned. My employer was so surprised—he told me later that he had expected the job to take a couple of days—that he gave me two five-dollar gold pieces and two silver dollars. Never before, nor since, have I felt quite so wealthy— nor quite so sure that I was the physical equal of any living man.

"Like most farm boys, I grew up believing that will-ingness and ability to work are the basic ingredients of successful farming. Hard, intelligent work is the key. Use it, and your chances for success are good. As an adult, this principle deepened into one of the main-springs of my life."

Over the years, as the Benson family grew, the house and the outbuildings on the farm were expanded. The cherished willow tree grew too. Year after year the family marveled at the endless new shoots the tree sent forth.

Like the Benson family itself.

The Bensons were part of everything important in that part of the world. Part of President Benson's love for the place is his love for its history. His ancestors figure prominently in it.

Explains President Benson: "I remember hearing a story about a community meeting that Grandfather was conducting. A new [church] unit was to be established, and Grandfather George T., Sr., asked what it should be named. One of the old pioneers said, 'Brother Benson, I don't know what you want to call it, but to us it is Paradise.' 'That's good enough,' said Grandfather. The name stuck.

"Now let me tell you about my beloved Whitney," continues President Benson. "There was one ward in Preston. Grandfather was a counselor in the bishopric. They decided there were enough farmers in the area where we lived to justify a unit. They called the priesthood together. Again the question was raised, 'What shall we call the new unit down there? What name shall we give this new ward?'

"Grandfather spoke up and said, 'There's a young bishop in Salt Lake whom I have often admired. He's a bishop of the Twentieth Ward and his name is Orson F. Whitney. I suggest we call this new ward the Whitney Ward.' And so it was. That's how Whitney got its name."

Later, as a member of the Quorum of the Twelve, Orson F. Whitney presided over the European and British missions when Ezra Taft was a young Elder in England. It was Elder Whitney who later performed the marriage ceremony for Ezra Taft and popular Flora Amussen.

"Elder Whitney knew about family love," says President Benson. "People ought to get hold of a little book he wrote just for his own family and had printed in a limited edition. It's called *Through Memory's Halls* and is one of the sweetest things that has ever been written for a family. President Whitney used to tell us missionaries how it was he went on a mission and how his life was changed because of it.

"As a young man Orson F. Whitney was active in the Pioneer Historical Society and wanted to make this work his lifetime career. He had it in his mind to go East to study. In those days going East was almost the same as apostatizing."

President Benson tells how Orson pleaded with his mother to help him pursue his ambition. She was a widow and had strong reservations about the whole idea, but he kept coaxing her until finally she said that she had a vacant lot and if they could sell it, she'd give him the money to go. Then she started praying earnestly to the Lord that the lot wouldn't sell. Time passed, and the family went to general conference. In those days it was the custom for President Brigham Young to read out the list of names of the missionaries and their assignments in the field. They were not interviewed; they just heard about the call at conference. At that conference Orson F. Whitney's name was read, and his field of labor was to be Pennsylvania.

"Elder Whitney went East," chuckles President Benson, "but not to study."

Young Whitney was a gifted writer, and he began sending stories back to Salt Lake from the East to be published in the *Herald*. It seems he was spending more time writing than proselyting. It was during this mission that Elder Whitney had the remarkable experience that changed his life and that deeply impressed young Ezra Taft Benson when he heard the story told again and again by his mission president. This experience has been recorded as follows:

"It was a dream, or a vision in a dream, as I lay upon my bed in the little town of Columbia, Lancaster County, Pennsylvania. I seemed to be in the Garden of Gethsemane, a witness of the Savior's agony. I saw Him as plainly as I have seen anyone. Standing behind a tree in the foreground, I beheld Jesus, with Peter, James and John, as they came through a little wicket gate at my right. Leaving the three Apostles there, after telling them to kneel and pray, the Son of God passed over to the other side, where He also knelt and prayed. It was the same prayer with which all Bible readers are familiar: 'Oh my Father, if it be possible, let this cup pass from me; nevertheless not as I will but as Thou wilt.'

"As He prayed the tears streamed down His face, which was toward me. I was so moved at the sight that I also wept, out of pure sympathy. My whole heart went out to Him; I loved Him with all my soul, and longed to be with Him as I longed for nothing else.

"Presently He arose and walked to where those Apostles were kneeling—fast asleep! He shook them gently, awoke them, and in a tone of tender reproach, untinctured by the least show of anger or impatience, asked them plaintively if they could not watch with Him one hour. There He was, with the awful weight of the world's sin upon His shoulders, with the pangs of every man, woman and child shooting through His sensitive soul—and they could not watch with Him one poor hour!

"Returning to His place, He offered up the same prayer as before; then went back and again found them sleeping. Again He awoke them, readmonished them, and once more returned and prayed. Three times this occurred, until I was perfectly familiar with His appearance—face, form and movements. He was of noble stature and majestic mien—not at all the weak, effeminate being that some painters have portrayed; but the very God that He was and is, as meek and humble as a little child. All at once the circumstance seemed to change, the scene remaining just the same. Instead of before, it was after the crucifixion, and the Savior, with the three Apostles, now stood together in a group at my left. They were about to depart and ascend to Heaven. I could endure it no longer. I ran from behind the tree, fell at His feet, clasped Him around the knees, and begged Him to take me with Him.

"I shall never forget the kind and gentle manner in which He stooped, raised me up, and embraced me. It was so vivid, so real. I felt the very warmth of His body, as He held me in His arms and said in tenderest tones: 'No, my son; these have finished their work; they can go with me; but you must stay and finish yours.' Still I clung to Him. Gazing up into His face—for He was taller than I—I besought Him fervently: 'Well, promise me that I will come to you at the last.' Smiling sweetly, He said, 'That will depend entirely upon yourself.' I awoke with a sob in my throat, and it was morning." (As quoted in Bryant S. Hinckley, *The Faith of Our Pioneer Fathers*, 1956, reprint [Salt Lake City: Bookcraft, 1974], pp. 211–12.)

For Ezra Taft Benson this account was a source of motivation and direction in his own life, remaining sacred within his own heart as he grew from a boy of the land to a man of the Lord.

2

The Preparation

Immense have been the preparations for me,
Faithful and friendly the arms that have help'd me.
                                    —Walt Whitman

President Benson proudly recalls that Whitney,
Idaho, was named for Orson F. Whitney. "Whitney is
part of Franklin County, the oldest pioneer settlement in
the state of Idaho," he relates. "When the pioneers first
settled here, they assumed that this was still part of Utah,
or would be. When the final survey was made, however,

the agreed boundary line put Franklin County just inside of Idaho."

There is a pioneer monument on the Cub River, a branch of the Bear, in memory of those early people who suffered untold hardships, including bitter cold, starvation, and Indian attack. Elsewhere along the river is a Boy Scout camp dedicated by President Benson and Alden Barber, who was an executive with the National Council of the Boy Scouts of America. Mr. Barber came West for the event and pronounced the site along the Cub River the best location for a Scout camp that he had ever seen in all of his travels. The land, the river, the foliage, the hiking trails—these are some of the features that boys enjoy and that can be found in this area.

"It's no wonder I'm so fond of Scouting," explains President Benson in telling about this event. "One of my greatest joys as a boy and as a man (even today, if I could) was to get on a horse and go up into the mountains. I like to ride up a ways, tie up my horse, and then walk and think and enjoy nature. I love animals, especially horses, and usually managed to have my own riding horse. One special delight was going with my parents or friends on camping, fishing, and hunting trips. Such peace and inspiration came while on these trips—marveling at the handiwork of God in His creation! Not that it was all work and no play on our farm, you see."

As a young man Ezra Taft played basketball and softball; he went swimming, ice skating, and sledding; and he was fond of riding his horse as a form of recreation. "We did things that, to a boy such as I, were half work and half play—like trapping muskrats and rounding up cattle in the mountains."

In the winter Cache Valley held other delights for active youth. It is a place of great beauty, typical of mountain altitudes in northern climates. Here the snowy mountains on the east are pine-shadowed deep blue. In certain stretches gray clouds press low against the rimming range. In other sections fog banks ribbon the interfolding ridge. Storm clouds often veil the high peaks. The valley itself licks up against the foothills like a lake—but a lake of freshly-powdered pasture and stubbled grain instead of water.

In those days the river cut through the valley bottom and in winter was easily seen from a distance because the bushes that marked its path were leaf-bare. Wild animal tracks peppered the banks as the stream wound around the acres, past the corral fences, silo, and stock shelters, and behind the mills. It was an ice path that shimmered through the frosted reeds and shrubs, sometimes softening into shining ice sheets that floated under cottonwoods, past wild berry bushes, tamarisk, and sumac. Time and again it would slide past a whole stand of poplars, planted in rows as windbreak, at this season showing one thousand naked arms reaching, embracing the sky.

The air was especially fresh in the winter valley, pure and invigorating to the noble Benson boy. Air pollution was unheard of. The snow was white and deep. The only mode of travel in winter was by horse-drawn bobsled. Even if people had had cars, they wouldn't have been able to use them in such snow. But a person could get a strong team pulling a wagon on runners to go almost anywhere, according to President Benson. Bobsled races were common fun, and the horses seemed to get as excited as young Ezra Taft and his friends at the reins.

Down the runner-rutted road from the Benson farm was a cross section wide enough for a lively winter activity. And Ezra Taft was a moving force in it.

"Do you know what 'shining' is?" he asked me once. "Shining is a-whirling and a-whirling in a bobsled. Father always used to let us keep one team of horses sharp shod—the metal horseshoes sharpened so that they would sink into the snow and grip the ice. We'd use that team of horses to accomplish 'shining.' I'd hold the reins so the horses would stand on command, and the bobsled would just whirl around and around until the ground below was shined slick into ice. It was wonderful! I remember that we used to pile all the boys and girls into the back of father's sled. How they loved it!"

Laughter would shatter the frozen air—laughter and shouts from unspoiled farm youth, blessed more with chores than idle time, making such occasions the more rewarding.

Winter on that farm in Idaho was a choice time for more than just ice games. Winter allowed time for reading. The family would circle together to do schoolwork, handwork, and mending. Then before bed Father Benson would ask that one member of the family read aloud to the rest. He might choose an article from a Church publication, the scriptures, or a book such as the *Autobiography of Benjamin Franklin.*

Young Ezra was as interested in learning as he was in playing or turning farm chores into an adventure. He learned early on that reading held an excitement all its own, and, because time to read was limited on the farm, President Benson came to value that privilege highly and learned to use reading time wisely by choosing worthwhile material. He still believes that choosing a good book is important, remarking that if "we spend time reading a cheap book, we will be forced to pass by a choice one" (*The Teachings of Ezra Taft Benson* [Salt Lake City: Bookcraft, 1988], p. 321).

Every member of the Benson family who could do so helped with the chores and field work. The demands of the farm often required that Ezra Taft, as the oldest child, miss school in the fall until the harvest was in and leave school early in the spring to assist with the planting. But during stormy days, Sundays, and evenings in winter, there was some time for reading.

Later, a mature Ezra Taft Benson urged the youth of the Church to "cultivate the reading habit," and he shared two favorite quotations that he had memorized when he was very young. He said, "These two quotations regarding books greatly influenced me: 'Be as careful of the book you read as of the company you keep, for your habits and character will be influenced by the former as by the latter'; and 'Except a living man there is nothing so wonderful as good books.'" (*The Teachings of Ezra Taft Benson*, p. 321.)

There was school, of course.

Ezra started formal classwork at the age of eight and finished at fourteen. He was large for his age then and would have felt that his education was complete, given the traditions of the time, except for the influence of one teacher who happened to be his great-aunt.

"I am especially grateful to her," remembers President Benson. "She somehow managed to impress on us the importance of education, the means of obtaining it, and the value of planning our future, not just drifting."

So there came a day, after extensive planning, when Ezra was able to attend the Oneida Stake Academy in Preston, Idaho. There at the "beloved academy" young Benson proved an able student. One of his classmates was a boy named Harold B. Lee, and the two of them came to know each other well. On one occasion they were together in a chorus established for a special occasion by director Charles Engar. President Benson recalls that they sang the hymn "Brightly Beams Our Father's Mercy" on stage at the grand old academy in Preston. They played basketball for the academy too. Frequently there were evening dances. "Oh, how well I remember dancing on that shining floor," President Benson reminisces. "I can remember the music. How I loved the music and loved to dance!"

The Oneida Stake Academy had at least two outstanding graduates during this time. They were Ezra Taft Benson and Harold B. Lee. Harold B. Lee was in debate. Ezra Taft Benson was a basketball star.

President Benson recalls: "We used to take a basketball tour from Preston to Sugar City and play every town along the way that was willing to play us. First we had Coach Clyde Packer, who had been on the team that won the national championship at Chicago. He was well known and skilled. He was so well known that when Rexburg got their new gymnasium and needed a coach to go along with it, they hired Clyde away from us. But one of Clyde's former basketball players, Charlie Cutler, became our coach then."

President Benson's stories about those basketball playing days, as he recounts them with the flair of an athlete, are still part of the man. "The time came for our first game with Rexburg—the first meeting of our coach and his old teacher. It was a real game! The final score was only 34–33 in our favor, and most of the points were made by fouls. They used to let us fight it out, try to take the ball away from each other. We won the game by only one point, but it was a hard loss for them. They were good sports, though, and managed to get a fine team of horses and a bobsled to take us up to Sugar City the next night to play. As I recall they even cheered for us."

That proved to bring quite a bit of fame for the Oneida Stake Academy team. At Sugar City they beat their opponents soundly. The team's most challenging games were played in Shelley. There the only place they could play basketball in winter months was the drained swimming pool. "Can you imagine playing basketball in a swimming pool," asked President Benson, "where there were no out-of-bounds at each end? You would throw the ball, hit the wall and . . . well, it's different now, and no more fun either, I'm certain."

Whether as a farmer or as a leader, Ezra Taft Benson has always been a practical man. He has often underscored this aspect of his personal philosophy by quoting the adage "There is no free lunch." He counsels that to succeed, to be a better farmer, often a creative approach is the best route. Rearrange the fields, enlarge the crop, cooperate with other farmers, and work!

He has been a popular speaker all of his life because of his firmness of principle, his exuberant spirit, and his forthrightness. On one occasion he addressed a large crowd at a prayer breakfast for the National Cattlemen's Association. It was New Year's Day 1979 in Kansas City, Missouri. Among other things, President Benson emotionally expressed:

"I am grateful to the Lord for my heritage, that my lot has been cast with the rural people of America, those who live on the farms and ranches. These people are the salt of the earth. No group of people in this nation knows so well that as ye sow, so shall ye reap. We have not all learned this lesson yet in America.

"During most of the time that men have lived on this earth, they have eked out a bare existence without the blessings of freedom. During the last one hundred years under freedom, farm efficiency has advanced until in America we have the most efficient agriculture in all the world. In 1940 one American farmer produced enough food for himself and nine other people. Today one average American farmer produces enough for himself and over fifty other people. On our large mechanized farms, one worker produces enough for himself and one hundred others. . . .

"I have lived all the past years of this, the twentieth century. I have witnessed great changes in our beloved land. I have seen us literally come from the horse and buggy days to our state of marvelous technological advancements. I have traveled most of the countries of the world, in both government and my Church capacity. To say that America is a blessed nation—a prosperous nation—is an understatement. Truly we live in a nation quite exceptional as compared to other nations. Certainly God has prospered this people.

"In the meantime, we must not forget the Source of all our blessings—our prosperity, our wealth, our comforts, our freedom. We must not forget that it is by God's gracious hand that these blessings are preserved, and not by our own superior wisdom. This is a paramount truth we need to uphold."

President Benson recalls that he used to know all the farmers in Franklin County, Idaho, and had been on practically every farm there. In his youth he was as impressed by those people as he was by their land. They were his teachers, his classmates, his relatives, his Church leaders, and the families of his friends. They were good people, he recalls. It was a blessing for a boy such as himself to mingle with people who knew how to work and how to serve, and who understood a person's duty to God. It was a great start in character building, admits President Benson.

For example, there was the figure of Joseph A. Geddes, a school principal and prosperous builder who had half the town's buildings to his credit. The Bensons bought their home from Joseph Geddes's father, who was a brick mason. They are still amazed over the terms of that investment. They paid about $400 down and kept a contract for $3,300.

Ezra Taft Benson was the county agent and worked for less than five hundred dollars a year. As agent he was the principal adviser to the farmers. He counseled them on livestock breeding, feeding, management, crop problems, planting schedules—the whole farm operation. He taught them sound principles of life, along with the science of agriculture.

"I traveled the state of Idaho working for eight years," he recalls, "and at one point I got a fellowship for graduate training. I was given a leave and was within five months of a doctoral degree when I had to return. I tried to get an extension to my leave, but there had been commitments made to other members of the work force."

However, Ezra was told that if he'd come home maybe he could go back to Berkeley to finish his degree in a few years.

That day never came. Instead, he went to Washington, D.C., to serve as executive secretary of the National Council of Farmer Cooperatives.

Ezra Taft Benson, farm boy, had moved out into the public world. A place as well as people, experiences as well as beliefs, helped the boy become the man—what he now is and what he has accomplished in his life.

There was a farm in Idaho, and there was a child that went forth from that farm to become a notable family man and patriot, a man who would one day be called as the prophet of God.

One fragrant, sunny Sabbath a new Sunday School teacher in a Midway ward stood near the chalkboard while his class gathered. Summer is a time when visitors come to Midway, and new faces in the Gospel Doctrine class each week are part of the teacher's challenge. But when President and Sister Ezra Taft Benson and some of their children and their family members filed into the classroom, panic mounted in the heart of the teacher.

Gathering his composure, he spoke to this Apostle of God: "President Benson, we welcome you. It is a privilege to have you with us, but surely you can't expect me to teach with you in the class! Now I'd like to turn the time over to you. May I?"

President Benson flashed his warming smile and replied, "I am just a ward member come to learn from *you*, and I have brought my family with me. They have come to learn, too. But they can sing for you, if you like."

And sing they did, to the delight of the class.

Then Brother and Sister Benson spoke. A noble patriarch and a gentle yet strong mother told of their dreams for their posterity and of their gratitude for their ancestors, his people and her people. The mix was good, and their parenting methods had brought results. The proof was there before the class. Clearly the family members loved each other and the Lord. It was readily apparent that their interaction was lively and fiercely loyal. Their example made for an impressive Sunday School lesson.

Ezra Taft Benson is indeed a family man.

The opportunities that have come to him as a Church leader and a public servant have been shared with his wife and children as often as has been appropriate and possible. Whatever burdens have come because of the demanding life-style have been shouldered by his family as well. Family is what life is all about, according to this great leader. Even if they haven't always traveled with him, traditions have welded them together.

Once when President Benson was touring Europe, he spent a night in Interlaken, Switzerland, enjoying a program from the local Swiss people that included folk songs, yodeling, dances, and Swiss horn music. It made him homesick for a moment. He was struck again with the wide variety and yet amazing similarity of people around the world who are "of the land." "What a lovely countryside there is in Switzerland, with the farms high up on the mountain slopes," he said. "Every one of them is groomed to perfection by people who care."

During his remarks at the dedication of the Swiss Temple, Elder Benson had the remarkable awareness that some of his own family's Swiss ancestors, long since dead, were present.

But Switzerland wasn't Cache County, either. A family man has special pleasure in remembering the place where he was reared and the scenes that first became familiar to him. They lend substance to his being all of his life.

When a boy becomes a man and takes his place—admirably and thankfully—at the head of a family, a new home is established, new places of security are formed, and additional loved ones fill his heart. Such was the case for Ezra Taft Benson.

President Benson likes showing a particular painting of his dear wife and children, his own immediate posterity. It is an enormous canvas of the Ezra Taft Benson family gathered in a musical moment around a grand piano. A copy hangs in his office, the office he uses as President of The Church of Jesus Christ of Latter-day Saints.

In the early days when he served in President Dwight D. Eisenhower's cabinet as secretary of agriculture, he had to live alone for the first period of that assignment. The lovely Benson family home on Harvard Avenue in Salt Lake City, Utah, had to be sold and another house located in the vicinity of Washington, D.C. Meanwhile, there were family schedules to meet. The children were growing up and assuming responsibilities of their own. They couldn't be uprooted and toted along like baggage to meet the needs of their father's schedule. Though Ezra took office in January, school wasn't out until June. But Flora went East as often as she could and was present at the festivities surrounding the inauguration of President Eisenhower.

On one occasion, after the new secretary of agriculture had put his beloved wife on the plane for Salt Lake to attend to the tasks of preparing household goods for another move, Secretary Benson returned to his lonely "bachelor" apartment into which Flora had moved his things while she had been there.

"Everywhere I turned I saw evidences of Flora's thoughtfulness," recalls President Benson, "like the way she had arranged my clothes and other possessions in the closet, brought in food, placed family pictures here and there, and left a loving note where I could see it before retiring.

"And then, for the first time, it was suddenly more than I could bear. The job ahead seemed too big, the load too heavy, loneliness too sharp a pain. I broke down and wept aloud."

One of the fine qualities of Ezra Taft Benson valued by people who know him well is his quick appreciation for those who have supported, sustained, counseled, or in any way aided him during the various stages of his preparation to become an important contributor to society.

And his beloved Flora is a most significant supporter among that number of the "faithful and friendly" people who have helped him.

3

The Awakening of Love

I know where I'm going,
And I know who's going with me,
I know who I love,
But the dear knows who I'll marry.
—Author unidentified

The awakening of love in the life of Ezra Taft Benson
came when he was about twenty years old. That was
when he met Flora Amussen.

People enjoy hearing the Bensons tell their courtship
story because it seems such a romantic one—quite

perfect and rare, rich because of the quality of the two friends involved.

It was love at first sight, they say. It has been lasting love from 1920 to the time of this writing. Their relationship has flourished through episodes of lengthy separations necessitated by a demanding schedule, as well as through experiences such as surviving a honeymoon in a leaking tent and scrimping to pay education debts. Together they have endured the stressful life of the public servant with its criticism and adulation in turn, the demands of glamorous gatherings, and the heady experience of keeping company with royalty and heads of state. Add to these the unusual pressures of the consuming commitment to high Church positions and the demands of a growing family, and the challenge is clear. Self-sacrifice and self-control had to be part of their lives too, if Flora and Ezra's young dreams of a peaceful, loving, God-fearing family unit were to be realized.

How did it all begin?

President Benson tells the beginning in his own delightful way: "The first time I saw Flora was early in the fall quarter of 1920. I was visiting a cousin who was registered at the Utah State Agricultural College [now Utah State University] in Logan, Utah. At the time I was planning to come down to Logan for the winter term which, because of my obligations on the farm, would be only my second quarter of college work in more than two years since I had finished high school. My brother Orval and I alternated college terms so that one of us would always be available on the farm. While my cousin and I were standing on the curb on Main Street, a girl drove by in a car and waved pleasantly to the boy at my side. A few minutes later she returned, repeating the greeting.

" 'Who's that?' I asked.

" 'That's Flora Amussen.'

" 'Well,' I said with the cockiness of youth, 'when I come down here this winter, I'm going to step her.'

"My cousin scoffed, 'Like heck you will. She's too popular for a farm boy!'

" 'Makes it all the more interesting.' "

Ezra Taft knew in his heart that he would do more than "step her." He felt that he would marry her some day. How it would come about he wasn't sure, but there was a small voice within him that marked her in his mind even though he didn't know her.

For Flora's part, she knew that there was someone new and very interesting-looking standing with her friend on the corner. A few weeks later Flora "happened" to visit Ezra's home ward in Whitney for church meetings. She was the house guest of one of his girl cousins.

It was fall and the aspen burned gold up the mountainside through red oak brush and patches of pine. It was Ezra's turn to work the farm. Not until winter quarter would he be back at Utah State in Logan.

What does a good young man think of as he is herding cattle, turning sod, reaping, harvesting? What feelings surge through his heart as he leans on a hoe and takes his rest looking toward a hill that stands apart on the horizon? This hill is a landmark. It is the lookout where his grandfather took his turn to watch through the night, his bride alone in their little cabin in the valley below. Indians on the prowl meant settlers would need a warning.

A thoughtful grandson contemplates the sacrifice and courage of his forebears and the duty to protect loved ones. And he dreams his own dreams for his own world someday.

Marriage—like Grandpa and Grandma's. *Struggle*—like Mother and Father starting out in a two-room place of their own making. People could be happy wherever they lived. *Building a kingdom*—like Great-grandfather, for whom he was named and who was obedient to a prophet's call to move West, to settle, and to serve wherever and whenever.

Good people. Great examples. Important goals.

Pleasant dreams for a fine young man. But what kind of a girl does a man need in order to live out a dream, to build a fine lifetime and an eternity? Why, with the right girl a man could make his life's mission a worthy one and have a great deal of joy along the way. But she had to be able to do things. A man couldn't sit and look at a pretty face all the rest of his life.

Of course, if she happened to be lithe and lovely, all the better!

He was glad his uncle had thought it was a good idea that Ezra take all the girls for a ride after church on that Sunday that Flora Amussen had visited their ward.

Flora and Ezra had their first date early that winter, shortly after young "T," as he was called by his family and friends, registered for school. They moved steadily in the direction of marriage; only, with life being what it is, it took them six years to reach that goal.

They each had some things they needed to do at this precious time of preparation in their lives. An early marriage in those days would have been extremely diffi-cult and limiting to their individual development. They realized this.

First things first.

There is a time and a season.

So they waited. And waited. A few letters and fewer visits managed to fan the flames.

What was the attraction between these two that allowed this relationship to flourish in spite of somewhat different backgrounds?

President Benson suggests that while education and a mission were equally important to both of them, other similarities seemed less obvious. Flora was from a three-story house filled with refining influences. Ezra was from a working farm filled with chores. His background was sheltered in a valley marked with willows, wagons, and close cousins for friends.

"The attraction between us was evident from the first," President Benson recalls, "but the contrast between us was extreme. She owned her own car and was actually the most popular girl in town; I was a farm boy in the traditional blue serge Sunday suit, typically shiny in the back. But she had, and never lost, a rare graciousness that put me immediately at ease."

Her charm and his warm appreciation of people have always been a strong part of their appeal.

Flora's soft eyes and modest manner concealed a lively mind and a firm testimony. She was petite, graceful, feminine, and directed. As a girl, she was a good sportswoman, was active in drama, and grew into a competent, energetic homemaker, a determined, prayerful mother, and a faithful support to a young comer, Ezra Taft Benson.

He was handsome with a fine-shaped, large head, ears pressed close to the scalp, chin strong, and eyes serious, searching, or brightly twinkling—depending! His full lips easily reflected his mood, the easy lift to his right eyebrow underscoring it. His hands were the strong hands of a man of the land, but with length and grace that were beautiful to watch when he'd slide his trombone on a musical program.

In college she became a singles tennis champion, an accomplished actress, and a student officer. He graduated from Brigham Young University with honors, and his fellow students voted him Most Popular Man. Of course they were attracted to each other.

He went to England on his mission and she went to Hawaii on hers. Their relationship deepened through a dance or two, school programs, regular church meetings, and a few letters sent to each other from far places. Time together was short and separation long, yet the attraction from the first moment remained. Each felt life was worth living with a long-range view. Each had worthy goals to reach and an abiding faith in God. Each felt that the other was worth waiting for.

Finally, apartness became togetherness forever. Ezra had earned a scholarship for graduate study at Iowa State College (later Iowa State University). He wrote to Flora to see if she would become part of the adventure. They had waited long enough. Says President Benson, "We had heard somewhere that two can live as cheaply as one." He wrote Flora and strongly hinted he would like her to go with him to Iowa as his wife. "When she answered my letter, I knew that I had won the only popularity contest that would ever really count."

The privileged girl who came from a life of wealth became a partner with an ambitious farm boy who took her East in a well-used Ford truck. He showed her how to camp out at night. He had always loved Scouting, the out-of-doors, and camping. She loved him and so it seemed a good arrangement. At least they were alone together, at long last.

They were married in the Salt Lake Temple on September 10, 1926, with Elder Orson F. Whitney officiating at the ceremony. That same day they started out on their honeymoon-camp-out, destination Iowa and all eternity.

The Awakening of Love

In Ames, Iowa, they found their accommodations just a step above their roadside camps with leaking tent and lumpy bed. They had their own room in the Lincoln Apartments, but they shared the facilities down the hall with three other couples.

These were years of privation as well as joy. Almost everything they did was an adventure, even finding food to eat. They recall stretching their meager food budget by gathering walnuts and drying them in the attic of the apartment building. Dried walnuts became such a staple in their diet during these student days that a slice of nut bread or a piece of walnut cake now can stir up a host of memories.

From Iowa it was back to Whitney. The graduate agricultural expert was to try his newfound techniques on the family farm. Now it was coal stoves and cows for Flora, babies in a row, gardening, canning, and bracing against hard winters. One of the most exciting moments in her life in those last days was getting electricity in the house and a stove to go along with it for proper baking.

Over the years the Bensons have had a dozen homes in at least five cities, with six children to ring the rafters. Sister Benson has been pleased with her family at each stage of their development. On one occasion, after her family was grown, she visited with a young mother of six children who listened as Flora told of how well the Bensons got along, how there was peace and no contention among them. The young mother sighed a deep sigh and admitted that her own six children often tried her patience severely because of their frequent quarrels.

"Train them to love each other, that's all," smiled Sister Benson. "You teach them to walk. Teach them how to get along." I was that young mother and have never forgotten that lesson.

Some years after leaving Whitney, the Bensons

entertained over a hundred young people for a Sunday night fireside in their Washington, D.C., home. Elder Benson spoke to them, and Sister Flora and their daughters served homemade Christmas treats. Afterward the whole family pitched in to clean up, as was their custom, while singing Christmas carols to soften the kitchen duty. Singing through their chores has always been a secret weapon to keep spirits sweet in their home. It isn't that the Bensons didn't have problems as a growing family; the message is clear that they learned how to deal with them appropriately.

4

Together, Together

There was a child went forth every day,
And the first object he look'd upon,
   that object he became. . . .
His own parents, he that had father'd him and she that
   had conceiv'd him in her womb and birth'd him,
They gave this child more of themselves than that,
They gave him afterward every day, they became
   part of him.

—Walt Whitman

Let's go back and take a closer look at that farm boy who became a prophet. What relationships throughout his life moved him in this remarkable direction and guided his deep feelings about families and eternal ties with loved ones extending in ever-widening circles?

There were his father and mother, George T. and Sarah Dunkley Benson, who made their mark on young Ezra. There were grandparents and uncles, aunts and cousins who enriched his life so much that now he hopes his own grandchildren can be blessed in similar ways.

"There was Uncle Serge. He was a presence in my life for a lot of reasons," explains President Benson. "Uncle Serge had a store and then sold it to Uncle Frank so that it was kept in the family—like the farm lands. That store played a major part in all our celebrations."

The family would gather with Ezra's mother's side or his father's side on alternating holidays. "If we had Thanksgiving at the Dunkleys'," he recalls, "we'd have Christmas feasting at the Bensons'. Next year we'd turn it around. But always Uncle Serge would come over from the store with a washtub full of presents. Every child was to get a present. No one was disappointed, just thankful for Serge and his store.

"It wasn't much but it was something. We'd be just as excited over what somebody else got for a present as we were with our own gift. It was how we were trained. It wasn't just the fact of a present, it was the surprise, the sharing, the delight in loving and in being in each other's company, too. Now that's Christmas!"

Summers too were for families in Whitney. There used to be an unwritten law that everyone in the area would take Saturday afternoon off during the summer. They'd all go down to a big pasture area reserved for a weekend "buckaroo." They'd play ball. There would be calves for the children to ride, races to run, and picnic food with raspberry juice. President Benson's memories include applauding family members when they would perform. There was a pair of twins, the Lowe brothers, who would do special musical numbers, and since they were the only set of twins in the town, they were of real interest.

Highlights of the Saturday activities included watching young Ezra participate. He was enthusiastic and a tough competitor. He liked winning. He liked excelling.

And he liked driving a car.

The well-used road between Preston, Idaho, and Logan, Utah, was dirt and gravel, except for the small stretch from Smithfield into Logan. President Benson recalls: "Once I got the old Dodge and went driving along that strip. It was too much to resist, that smooth paving. Well, I got that old car up to fifty-one miles per hour. That was the fastest that car ever had gone, and it was the talk of the whole town. It was the most dangerous thing any of them had ever heard of, too."

Ezra Taft Benson was full of life—a dependable, obedient, hard-working young man, but always full of life. He wanted to learn. He was exuberant with the adventure of living, season changes, life cycles, and relationships. Take courting, for example. President Benson has told his family members many times about the difference between courting in a buggy and courting in an automobile.

"People used to refer to my father, George T. Benson, Jr., and my mother, Sarah Dunkley Benson, as the ideal couple in the community. But Father had to go a long way to court Mother. He didn't have a car then, either. Mother's family home was about three miles by buggy, but, if he wanted to see her very often, he would have to walk both ways. People said they could always tell if things went well on his visits to the Dunkleys' because on the way back he'd be whistling or singing." President Benson also remembers that whenever his father had been away from his wife and family, he'd always come back whistling or singing. "Mother would have the bread and milk ready for him, too. They were a good example."

Bread and honey was Ezra's boyhood treat. A friend introduced it to him as they walked home from school. It became a pattern, for a time, for Ezra to stop at his friend's house on the way home from school. He was so grateful for the offering of bread and honey before the long walk ahead to the Benson farm with the inevitable chores waiting.

Naturally it became a tradition all the years after to sweeten life with the same late-day treat. There has been a slight modification in the recipe, however, according to President Benson. He combines the best of two worlds from his past. A thick slice of whole wheat bread "drizzled generously with honey and swimming in milk" is a comfort to a farm boy grown sophisticated through graduate degrees and worldwide work.

The family always regarded this treat as acceptable; but they had difficulty understanding it when he'd garnish this milk and honey dish with fat, sliced, raw onions!

It became a family ritual and joke for Father Benson to come into the kitchen and pick a choice whole onion. He would check it over and then, as if it were an apple, he would take a big bite out of it.

"I love onions," exclaims President Benson, "but the children questioned this method I had of eating them. I'd bite that onion and then look at it with real satisfaction and then smile at the wondering faces of my family. Together they would mock me with the phrase they'd heard over the many years of this ritual, 'You know, the onion is the most neglected vegetable in the world!' "

Good food is part of the Benson heritage to the
present time. When the Bensons speak of good food,
they aren't talking about rich gourmet dishes full of
destructive sugar and fat; rather, they mean food that
comes fresh from the soil and is prepared with the
delicate hand of one who values natural flavor and
nutrition. The care of the body is, as the care of the
spirit is, an important part of the Benson family training.

"The man who cannot learn from the past will be a
poor steward of the future," President Benson has taught
on many occasions. It is a running theme in his family
training, too. He has said: "The lessons of history stand
as guideposts to help us safely chart the course for the
future. They affirm again how far-reaching are the
effects of daily decisions—yours and mine—upon
generations yet unborn." (See *The Teachings of Ezra
Taft Benson,* p. 701.)

This principle applies, of course, to women as well.
President Benson has such affection and admiration for
his wife that he feels all young women, not just his own
posterity, can learn from her example. When Flora A.
Benson was cited as Woman of the Year by the Lambda
Delta Sigma sorority at the University of Utah, she was
introduced with this statement from her husband: "Certainly she has taken her family responsibilities most
seriously. She has played, sung, cried, and studied with
[our children] and considered faithfully their every
need. Her great faith knows no bounds. When problems
arise, she always goes to the Lord in prayer—usually
with the family, and often in a special prayer with those
most directly concerned. She has instilled in all her
children a strong testimony of the gospel, and to me she
has always been a constant inspiration."

Over the years of public life the Benson family has
made it a point to remain stalwart and courageous
proponents of the Mormon life-style, of the philosophy

39

and doctrine of The Church of Jesus Christ of Latter-day Saints.

When Sister Flora was hostess in the Benson home to First Lady Mamie Eisenhower and the wives of the members of the Eisenhower cabinet, it was a luncheon beautifully appointed in every way but in keeping with high personal standards of nutrition and the Word of Wisdom, standards for which the Benson family had become known in political circles.

On that occasion Sister Benson explained to her guests, "Now, you will find some things different in our home. There will not be any tobacco; there will not be any cocktails or liquor. There will not be any tea and coffee, but we'll try to make it up to you in our way." Flora came from a home where entertaining was done with beautiful accessories and in a gracious manner for the comfort of guests. She was equal to any company, and she fussed over these lovely women in the Benson home that particular day and other dignitaries on other days. The family never suffered because of their strict ideals, and many learned important lessons from their example over the years. One newspaper in Pennsylvania reported:

"We will take Ezra Taft Benson without a martini in his hand to any other public official with one. We prefer men of distinction who got that way without a cocktail calling card. We like the image of Washington we learned from the schoolbooks. We deplore the preference of some for martini-government. We think it is time officials who have the courage of their convictions against such goings-on be told they have friends and supporters back home."

For the Bensons, family togetherness has gone beyond food, music, Church service, and entertaining friends. They have always helped each other with preparations for public appearances, whether at school, before Congress, or at a general conference of the Church, as Barbara Benson Walker did in singing her father's favorite song at the meeting in which he was sustained President of the Church.

Some years ago the family of Ezra Taft and Flora Amussen Benson was featured with Edward R. Murrow on his weekly television show. That particular production received the most fan mail of any in the history of that program.

Wherever the Bensons have lived, they've prepared a home where guests of any age have always been welcome. Over the years these guests have included close friends of the family as well as distinguished citizens. One of their favorite memories is of the excitement they felt in presenting a family home evening for the president of the United States, Dwight D. Eisenhower, and his wife, Mamie.

Badminton and croquet outside and a Ping-Pong table inside were a fundamental part of the Bensons' home furnishings. Sandbox, swings, and a shuffleboard court were as important as flowers and a vegetable garden—all of which were vital to both Ezra and Flora. Recreation was a high principle of life for all of them, and it eased the strain of demanding schedules.

"I've always liked to sing and used to be a soloist," President Benson explains. "When the children were young, we had a juke box for them in our recreation room so that good music was available for our family dances too." Once a week the family gathered to sing and to play their instruments and also to dance waltzes and polkas together. Laughter echoed through whatever house they were filling at the time.

Here again is proof of the strong influence the past life of Ezra Taft Benson has had upon his present. He has reached back into early family traditions and found a way to instill these valuable ideas and opportunities into the lives of his own children as well as others who might come under his influence.

Dancing was a tradition, along with prayer.

"We always used to have our dances with both the parents and the young people enjoying the time together," says President Benson. "I loved to dance and I learned to dance the waltz with Mother. Our sons learned to dance with their mother, too. Oh, those old dances in the basement of the church were wonderful. We used to dance around and around the poles that supported the chapel. Even Grandma danced. She was Scottish, and how we enjoyed watching her dance the Highland fling!"

President Benson shared these memories when the Church was planning its sesquicentennial celebration and the suggestion was made that a family ball be held. He was enthusiastic about the idea. When the time came, he and his Flora were graceful leaders of one flank of the grand march, and they danced well and long in tuxedo and formal, obviously still so much in love.

As for the Scottish grandmother, she taught Ezra more than dancing. She taught him the joy that comes from gardening and sharing the fruits and flowers. "When Grandmother and Grandfather had finished farming after their children were all gone from home," President Benson recalls, "they moved into a big home with a porch on three sides and a garden of flowers surrounding the whole of it. It was the beauty spot of the whole community. I've seen Grandmother go to the ward with her arms full of flowers, spring or fall. Somehow she managed her planting to keep that ward full of flowers."

Family solidarity was another principle from his childhood that was cultivated for the blessing of his own posterity. Flora and Ezra preached *together* and trained *together*, so that, even though the children have been scattered, reunions are important. The singing, the dancing, the laughing, and the praying with each other go deep into the next generation as well.

President Benson speaks tenderly of his own parents: "My parents, required to be frugal, were industrious, and the love of God that was in their hearts overflowed into their life. They sincerely appreciated the opportunity of parenthood, and they really worked hard to generate in their eleven children (I was the oldest) habits of honesty, industry, and 'doing your job,' whatever it might be. The idea that each of us, besides being an individual, was a member of a social unit—the family—was so deeply ingrained that as a family, as the roadside posters came to say, we sang together, played together, prayed together, worked together, and stayed together. We were encouraged to bring our friends home with us as well. What a time we would have popping corn and singing! Mother had a way of always making our friends welcome as part of the group."

In each phase of Ezra Taft Benson's career there has been no way other than to have all the family included. Everybody together always is how the Bensons like life best, and now this tradition has been carried down to the grandchildren and great-grandchildren.

5

Flora

If you your lips would save from slips,
Five things observe with care:
Of whom you speak, to whom you speak,
And how, and when, and where.
                    —Author unidentified

Sister Flora Benson has always suggested that when one member of the family is in the public eye serving mankind, all of the family is on inspection. All the family should set proper examples, too.

Flora Amussen Benson was the youngest daughter of Carl and Barbara Smith Amussen. Her mother was born in Tooele and her father in Köge, Denmark, a descendant of a distinguished Danish ancestry.

Carl Amussen became very successful as a jeweler and watchmaker during the gold rush of 1848 in Australia. Events occurred that brought him in touch with the missionaries, and he responded to the invitation for baptism. After he joined the Church he came to America. It was 1865, and opportunities for success were strong. Carl opened a jewelry business on Main Street in Salt Lake City, Utah, where the Crossroads Mall now fills the block across from Temple Square. However, for the better part of a century the Amussen building was a landmark, and for Flora it was a tender, public reminder of the father who had died when she was only a year old, the youngest of seven children born to Barbara, his third wife.

Barbara Amussen reared these children herself, and, by the time Ezra Taft Benson came to know her, she had grown in strength and wisdom. He loved her deeply. He valued her counsel and her perspective on the gospel. He found he could talk with her about subjects he was studying in the university. His repeated use of the remarkable stories about his mother-in-law indicates the place she had in his extended circle of loved ones— people who have added dimension to his life.

Barbara Amussen, Flora Benson's mother, lived to enjoy the gift of foreseeing and understanding future events. Among other things, it came to her that her son-in-law, Ezra Taft Benson, would, in due time, serve in a high and important calling in the "glorious Church." She also announced to her family beforehand the date on which she would take leave of this life. It had been made known to her through a visitation from her deceased husband, and she made the necessary preparations.

President Benson says that during the early part of the week in which she died she told her eldest daughter, Mabel, "The Lord has just made it known to me through my husband that my time has come, that on Thursday it will all be over—I will have passed on." Since her mother seemed in such good health, Mabel tried to dissuade her. Unfortunately, this conversation did not impress the daughter enough at the time for her to notify family members.

But the mother insisted that she was not afraid of this natural part of one's experience on earth. She knew what she had to do to be ready, and she went about doing it. She withdrew money from the bank and bought her own casket. She paid off her debts and made arrangements in the early part of the week with electricians and plumbers to have the power and water turned off on Friday. She bore her testimony so fervently during a Church meeting that people sat in reverent silence until the bishop finally closed the meeting. She asked her daughter if she could spend a couple of days with her. On Wednesday night she said that she felt weak and needed rest. The family members recall her last words, which were to this effect: "I am going to sleep now. I am weak and tired, but I feel happy in my heart. Don't wake me even though I sleep until the eventide." She didn't wake up again.

Family examples such as this have strengthened the faith of the Bensons. His own great-grandfather was a man of strength and faith and therefore a great example to which President Benson clings. That first Ezra Taft was an Apostle and a captain of ten in the first group of pioneers that entered the Salt Lake Valley in 1847. Subsequently he built a two-story home of showplace quality on the corner where Zion's Bank now stands in downtown Salt Lake. Just as he and his families were about to move from their log cabins into the new home, he was called on a mission to Cache Valley by President Brigham Young, who suggested that he sell the home to Daniel H. Wells, President Young's counselor. Ezra Taft's response was a great example to his descendant, the second Ezra Taft Benson. There was no murmuring. There was only acceptance and a moving forward in obedience, with a sense of the adventure of life that comes with responding positively to change and challenge. Cache Valley thus became the beloved home of the Bensons through the generations.

In a central place in President Benson's personal office is an oil portrait of his great-grandfather, the pioneer Ezra Taft Benson. The painting is a prized possession of President Benson and was a surprise gift to him some years ago when he attended a ribbon-cutting ceremony in Tooele, Utah, marking the restoration of the first Tooele grist mill, built by his great-grandfather. This first Ezra Taft Benson participated in the ceremonies when the Golden Spike was driven to join the east and west railroad lines, creating the first continental railroad. This colonizer also founded early cooperatives with a joint effort philosophy that, even today, President Benson admits is the basis for his own deep interest in people working together to accomplish end desires.

People with strength of character and purity of purpose weave a sense of security and infuse a desire for striving and building among those with whom they live. So it has been with the two Ezra Taft Bensons.

Holding up members of the family as examples to follow is a rite of parenthood with the Bensons. They have reached back through the generations along several family lines to find excellent examples in problem solving, personal progress, Christlike service, devotion to duty, and loyalty to country and clan. In this way, a closeness to God and a love of country—traits which inspire one to keep the law of God and of the land— naturally take root in family members' hearts; their development is expected, not just hoped for.

Ezra Taft and Flora Amussen Benson are the parents of six children. They have thirty-four grandchildren and, at this writing, almost three dozen great-grandchildren.

Some years ago, with his family gathered about him in a public setting, President Benson received a glowing tribute from Meade Alcorn, who said: "I would like to pay tribute here in his home state to a great American— a man who has become a national symbol of unflinching courage and unwavering conviction. We don't often see his like."

Many other honors and considerations for high office and wealthy employment have come to Ezra Taft Benson over the years, but Church service and family service have been his greatest joy and first concern, and he admits that he doesn't know where one ends and the other begins, so closely are family and service to God intertwined.

Life, as well as some of God's children, has a way of keeping a public person on his knees, according to President Benson, but he has developed the kind of humorous perspective that is suitable for days of honor as well as days of trial.

He has a favorite story that he has repeated often over the years. It concerns a businessman who came home after his day at the office and, as he greeted his wife, said enthusiastically, "My dear, you will never guess what happened to me at the office today."

She said, "No, I am sure I can't guess, but it must have been wonderful; you look so happy."

"Yes, my company made me a vice president."

Ezra Taft and Flora Amussen Benson

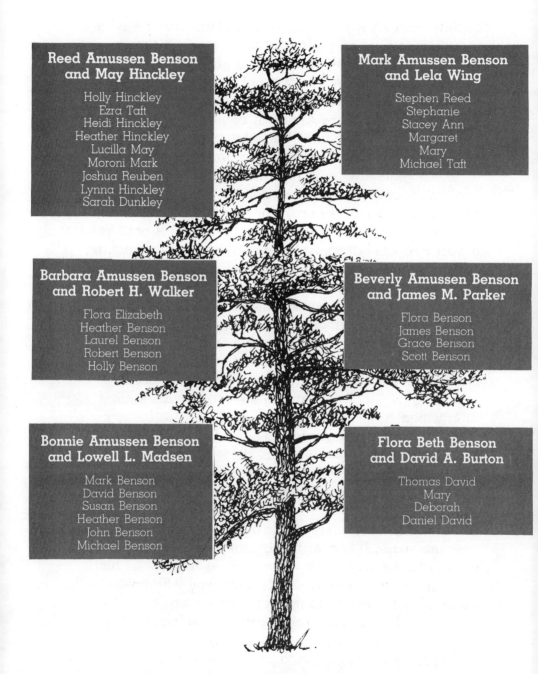

Reed Amussen Benson
and May Hinckley

Holly Hinckley
Ezra Taft
Heidi Hinckley
Heather Hinckley
Lucilla May
Moroni Mark
Joshua Reuben
Lynna Hinckley
Sarah Dunkley

Mark Amussen Benson
and Lela Wing

Stephen Reed
Stephanie
Stacey Ann
Margaret
Mary
Michael Taft

Barbara Amussen Benson
and Robert H. Walker

Flora Elizabeth
Heather Benson
Laurel Benson
Robert Benson
Holly Benson

Beverly Amussen Benson
and James M. Parker

Flora Benson
James Benson
Grace Benson
Scott Benson

Bonnie Amussen Benson
and Lowell L. Madsen

Mark Benson
David Benson
Susan Benson
Heather Benson
John Benson
Michael Benson

Flora Beth Benson
and David A. Burton

Thomas David
Mary
Deborah
Daniel David

THE BENSON FAMILY TREE

"Well, that's wonderful, dear, but you know vice presidents are pretty common these days."

"Common? They are not common."

"Yes, they are," she said. "There is a wholesale grocer here in town that has a vice president in charge of prunes."

"That can't be right."

"It *is* right."

It bothered the man all the way to the office the next day. Determined to find out, he called the wholesale grocer and said to the operator, "I want to talk to the vice president in charge of prunes."

"Surely," said the girl. "Packaged or bulk?"

Sister Flora Benson has always had a way of listening that has brought about the softening, the comforting, or the enlightening that Ezra Taft Benson has seemed to need at the moment. But she has helped in other ways too.

During his demanding and often truly difficult years as secretary of agriculture in the Eisenhower cabinet, the battles to straighten out the farm programs of the nation had the secretary on the firing line.

"It had always been my characteristic to determine an objective and then drive directly at it with no detours," President Benson points out. "One day President Eisenhower talked about this characteristic of mine and the difficulties it engendered when applied to political realities.

"The president took a pad of paper and with a black pencil marked a bold *X* at the top of the paper. At the bottom he drew a rough square. Then he explained that in the military there is always a major objective. He pointed to the *X* and said to consider it as the objective while the square represented the forces. Then he said: 'It might seem that the simplest thing to do is to go straight toward the objective. But that is not always the best way to get there. You may have to move to one side or the other. You may have to move around some obstacle. You may have to feint, to pull the defending forces out of position. You may encounter heavy enemy forces and temporarily have to retreat. There may be some zigs and zags in your course as you move toward the objective. That may have to be the way you work at this farm problem.' "

Secretary Benson went home to talk it over with Flora. He was a learner and she a good listener. They realized that they would have to begin with the elements that they had at hand; they would have to work with the people of America themselves in order to help the farmer. He would have to take his message out to the country and count on Flora, as usual, to hold down the home front and be with the family.

However, Flora did make a few public appearances with prepared and off-the-cuff remarks. And each time she did, she won friends for her husband and his cause. She was cited positively by the media for her speaking skill and style. Her training in drama at school and her missionary experience for the Church served her well.

Through it all, from their courtship and marriage days to his sacred calling as President of The Church of Jesus Christ of Latter-day Saints, Ezra Taft and Flora Benson have touched hearts, held hands, and held on to each other. And to God.

Perhaps it wasn't just because President Benson is a very important person that the new class teacher in the Midway ward Sunday School felt nervous. It may be that President Benson exudes life. He is a presence. His experiences and personal growth in life, coupled with his unique quality of character, account for his bursting confidence and sweet, disarming humility.

He is educated, energetic, and experienced, and he cares intensely about the right things. He cares about people. He is full of praise and quick to appreciate the efforts of others, traits which prove to be healing influences in the lives of others. The people say: "Come what may, everything will be all right when Ezra Taft Benson is in charge. Especially with Flora by his side."

6

The Son, The Leader

I'd rather see a sermon than hear one any day;
I'd rather one should walk with me than
    merely tell the way.

                    —Edgar A. Guest

The Benson family has a wide collection of homespun verses that they use to teach and train up persons of character. They have handed down the tradition from father to son, and from mother to daughter, that the way parents live influences mightily the way grown sons and daughters will handle their own families.

Ezra Taft Benson was a sensitive child and an obedient son, and he watched the lives of his parents closely. Their actions spoke louder to his heart than the familiar verses they taught or the scriptures they read. What he remembers is that his parents *did* read the scriptures. They *did* live by the principles of the gospel. They did not take the casual way.

He recalls, with a kind of wonder, the time he watched his parents face a crisis of personal sacrifice for Church service. As it turned out, his own life changed through the experience. He was twelve years old and was tending the little ones of the family while his parents attended sacrament meeting. The children in the community were not allowed to go that week because of a particular epidemic in the Whitney community.

On the way home from the meeting, George and Sarah stopped at the store where mail was delivered. After sacrament meeting the storekeeper would unlock his doors just long enough for the mail to be picked up by those who came in from the farms to go to church. No purchase of goods was allowed, but getting their mail then saved these people another trip.

There was a special letter waiting for George T. Benson, Jr. As he drove the buggy home, his wife read the letter. It was a mission call for him! It also was a surprise. No one had interviewed them to see if there were funds, if the household could manage without its head, or if they were even desirous of such an assignment. As to worthiness, the bishop was already aware of the worthiness of the ward families, especially in this case, since the bishop of George T. Benson, Jr., was George T. Benson, Sr.!

At home, Ezra's parents gathered the children around them. It was one of those poignant times of love and closeness that life presents. Both George and Sarah were weeping, President Benson recalls. The children had never seen both parents in tears at the same time. These were strong, albeit loving, people. These were tears of tenderness, however, not of reticence, questioning, or complaining. The parents explained to the children that their father had been called on a mission that would last almost two years.

This was a stunning announcement. Questions flew. Hearts pounded. The children followed their parents to kneel for family prayer. Then plans were made. A married couple could move into part of the house. In exchange for the board and room, they would be responsible for the row farm. But the large burden fell upon young Ezra because, four months after George arrived in the mission field, Sarah gave birth to her eighth child. The little children took care of the dairy herd, the hay, and the pastureland. Of course, neighbors and extended family members helped out during that two-year period.

This arrangement proved to be an important lesson and a keen preparation for the perceptive farm boy who one day would be a prophet of God. Young Ezra learned about work on a broader basis than ever before. He felt the burden of responsibility. What he did or failed to do made a difference. He came to understand accountability, too, as he reported regularly to his father through letters. But he became aware also of the great blessing and accomplishment that can be achieved when people help others.

When George returned to Whitney after serving his mission in the Chicago area, Ezra would sit near him on his own three-legged milk stool as they milked the cows morning and evening. He remembers these occasions with mighty joy and thanksgiving. Everything was going to be all right because Father Benson was home. Ezra knew his father was glad to be home too because, as soon as the milking began, so did joyful singing.

The son learned all the words to the Church hymns from his father, who sang them with gusto. And so did the boy. No half-hearted hymns in that household, or that milk barn. They sang "Ye Elders of Israel," "Israel, Israel, God Is Calling," "Come, All Ye Sons of God," "Ye Who Are Called to Labor," and so on.

This did more than teach a young boy hymns and bind a father and son together. The whole family was affected by the missionary zeal of a father who was willing to serve and a mother who was unmurmuring while he did. All seven sons filled missions at least once. All of the girls served missions, too, either with their husbands or as widows.

The father taught the son to pray, and President Benson remembers the reverence required before God as the family knelt together for this purpose. This training carried over into Ezra Taft Benson's whole life. To pray was much more than to recite needs or to list gratitudes. It was to commune with God in a worshipful way and to counsel with him concerning personal or family situations. As a student, as a young married man, as a responsible official of the United States government, and as an Apostle of God, Ezra Taft Benson has consistently followed a pattern of conversing regularly with Heavenly Father.

There is a picture that remains clear and a memory that is precious to many who were part of a large group of Mutual Improvement Association general board leaders. Despite the passage of nearly thirty years, that particular prayer meeting preceding June 1961 conference, when Ezra Taft Benson was the General Authority adviser, has remained a memorable one. A new Young Women presidency had been called. June conference had special challenges resulting from the calling of new board members, the exploding growth rate in Church membership, and the unrest among students. Many countries would be represented. New programs were being introduced to meet frightening trends infiltrating society.

The board members were anxious and in need of guidance. They came to the meeting fasting. They gathered in the board room of the old Presiding Bishopric office building that stood where pathways, fountains, gardens, and a high-rise building now mark the Church plaza block.

Elder Benson requested that the opening hymn be "I Need Thee Every Hour." He said it was a favorite of his. It was clearly a suitable song on such an occasion, when needs were great among leaders who were attempting to guide youth in trying times. Loving to sing himself, radiantly smiling to the humble, waiting group, Elder Benson joined in singing the hymn, and the presence of the Spirit was increasingly felt as each verse was sung. Elder Benson sang enthusiastically, setting an example of confidence before God. Prayer was to be led by Elder Benson. That was planned, but the announcement he made as he took his place at the podium was a surprise. He asked us all to kneel; a moment of reverence was allowed before the spirited and emotion-filled voice of Elder Benson addressed Heavenly Father in prayer. The powers of heaven were called forth. The needful, hopeful servants in the Church auxiliary system wept, as the Spirit swelled in the room through the importuning of this special witness of God.

It was a long prayer. It dealt with specifics. In his prayer Elder Benson remembered each department and committee—speech, drama, music, dance, athletics, age groups. He prayed for the leader and participants, the delegates and advisers, and the youth of the Church as well. He prayed for the elements and environments, the facilities, and the safety of all.

Elder Benson knew how to talk with the Lord. Nobody was in doubt about that. His life on the farm had taught him the value of faith in a God who could be counted on in solving the problems of harvest and herds. Strength came from family prayer.

Life was such in the Whitney area that Ezra's teachers at church and school were often his relatives. For example, Uncle Serge Benson was Ezra's teacher and underscored the family teachings in the classroom. Apart from Ezra's own father, his Uncle Serge was probably the man who made the most vivid and lasting impression on the Benson youth. President Benson recollects that Uncle Serge Benson taught more than the traditional classroom subjects; he also taught intellectual courage, honesty, integrity, and the value of taking a stand in defense of righteousness and truth, no matter what.

But there were some teachers along the way, not relatives, who may not have known about Ezra's strict home training and his characteristic obedient response. President Benson recalls: "One day in the middle of an important examination in high school, the point of my lead pencil broke. In those days, we used pocketknives to sharpen our pencils. I had forgotten my penknife, and turned to ask a neighbor for his. The teacher saw this. He accused me of cheating. When I tried to explain, he gave me a tongue-lashing for lying. Worse, he forbade me to play on the basketball team in the upcoming big game.

"I could see that the more I protested the angrier he became. But again and again I stubbornly told him what had happened. Even when the coach found out and pleaded my cause, the teacher refused to budge. The disgrace was almost more than I could bear. Then, just minutes before the game, he had a change of heart. And I was permitted to play. But there was no joy in it. We lost the game, and, though that hurt, by far the deeper pain was being branded a cheat and a liar.

"Looking back, I know that that lesson was God-sent. Character is shaped in just such crucibles."

Though the teacher didn't believe him, his own father did. Young Ezra began to realize that peace and respect from the right kind of people come only through a clear conscience. "Then, if misunderstanding or criticism and blame come, one is free to rise above it," he explains.

He also learned the importance of avoiding even the appearance of evil. He says: "Though I was innocent, circumstance made me look guilty. Since this could easily be true in many of life's situations, I made a resolution to keep even the appearance of my actions above question as far as possible. And it struck me too that, if this injustice happened to me, it could happen to others, and I must not judge their actions simply on appearances."

There came a time when young Ezra felt a yearning to receive a patriarchal blessing—to learn, through prayer and the laying on of hands by one in authority, what Heavenly Father had to say concerning his particular mission on earth. He wanted to know, for example, if he was meant to fill a mission. He had recently listened intently while two missionaries had reported their activities. It had seemed wonderful to him. So he talked with his father about getting such a blessing. His father explained that a person had to be worthy to receive a patriarchal blessing. "Am I worthy, Father?" the seventeen-year-old youth asked. "I think you are, son," the father replied, "but it's for the bishop to say. Why don't you go ask the bishop?" So Ezra had a brief interview over in a corner of the church and received an authorization from the bishop, who happened to be his grandfather, to receive a patriarchal blessing. This was on April 15, 1917.

It happened that Patriarch John Edward Dalley was visiting the ward that day, and young Benson approached him about an appointment. The gentle, older man at once invited Ezra to walk the distance with him to the home of a friend where the blessing could be given that very day. Patriarch Dalley walked with young Ezra up the country road to the appointed place. President Benson said that as Brother Dalley's hands were placed upon his head and the blessing commenced, his own inquiring spirit relaxed. He submitted to the power he felt through the priesthood that day. He was promised that, if faithful, he would go on a mission "to the nations of the earth crying repentance to a wicked world." He did, and that has been his cry in all the many years since, as he has traveled the earth encouraging people to become more righteous.

The familiar farms of Whitney seemed to disappear, and ground, so dear to a farmer lad, faded from beneath his feet as he made his own long walk back from that spiritual experience.

A young man on his first mission learns how to pray with effect. It is the avenue to success and sometimes to survival. President Benson has often talked to youth groups anticipating missions and shared the dramatic incident during his first mission when he and his companion were terrified by an angry mob in England. As they preached, the mob and the feelings of hostility swelled when someone identified the young preachers as

Mormons. The two missionaries became separated, and the mob began pushing them. Elder Benson began to pray fervently for help. "When it seemed that I could hold out no longer," he later recalled, "a big husky stranger pushed his way through to my side. He looked me straight in the eye and said in a strong, clear voice, 'Young man, I believe every word you said tonight.' " Just then an English bobby came forth and escorted him, and later his companion, safely back to their lodgings, where they knelt in a prayer of thanksgiving.

Ezra Taft Benson's life is full of incidents that testify of God's love and help for him over the long years of varied service. He himself knows that these choice experiences prove the goodness, the wisdom, and the caring of God.

From being a farmer's son to serving as a leader in high places, to guiding a lively family as a father, Ezra Taft Benson has chosen to live by faith and to seek to do the will of his Heavenly Father. And whether as a son or a leader, he has repeatedly remarked—in his unique, fervent way—that he has conscientiously tried never to do or say anything that would hurt or bring disgrace to his family or the Church.

7

The Patriot

Oh, beautiful for spacious skies,
For amber waves of grain,
For purple mountain majesties
Above the fruited plain!

. . . .

Oh, beautiful for heroes proved
In liberating strife,
Who more than self their country loved,
And mercy more than life!

    —Katherine Lee Bates

The preceding verses represent the America that Ezra Taft Benson has always loved. Throughout his boyhood in Whitney, Idaho, and throughout his service in the cabinet of the president of the United States, the sight of farmland could always rouse his patriotic fervor.

On one occasion while he was serving as secretary of agriculture, he stood on a rise in the flatlands of the Midwest. The grain fields stretched as far as his eyes could see. Past their early greening now, ripening shafts darkened near the horizon, and amber grain disappeared into a misty mirage.

It was beautiful to him. It wasn't Whitney, Idaho, but it was America, land of the free, land of promise. His heart swelled as he thought of the debt the people of this country owe to brave pilgrims, pioneers, settlers, loggers, miners, frontiersmen, and farmers. Yes, the farmers. With his eyes he scanned the waves of grain to the horizon, and he determined that surely the future would be bright for America if he had anything to do with it—for America, the promised land, and for its people. He would invest his energies in preserving this land, under God, for a righteous people. He remembered the words of William Penn: "Those people who will not be governed by God must be ruled by tyrants." Ezra Taft silently echoed the sentiment: "Government without God *is* tyranny."

Perhaps moments like this moved this great patriot to support changing the wording of the Pledge of Allegiance. The words, "under God," were later inserted to follow the words, "one nation." Now school children and all citizens recite the Pledge of Allegiance this way: "I pledge allegiance to the flag of the United States of America and to the Republic for which it stands, one nation *under God*, indivisible, with liberty and justice for all."

During the Church's participation in the celebration
of America's bicentennial, Elder Benson pointed out the
significant fact that, for all practical purposes, the
United States Constitution had been made binding on
April 6, 1789. He reminded the audience that April 6 is
also the Savior's birthday and the date of the organization of the Church. Surely this was not coincidental, he
said.

America. Farmland. Youth. Patriots. Scouting could
turn boys into patriots. Though Ezra had moved on to
become an Apostle of the Lord and to accept the post of
secretary of agriculture in Eisenhower's cabinet, Scouting still held a high place in his heart. Scouting could
turn boys into patriots!

It was several years ago that he took the assignment
of Scoutmaster of a troop of Scouts in his treasured
Idaho community. There were twenty-four boys and
twice that many challenges, it seemed, as he met with
them. President Benson looks back on that time as a
precious enrichment that would affect the rest of his life,
wherever his community, Church, or family responsibilities might take him.

One time his troop was to compete in a special stake
activity. Each ward was to have a boys' chorus. Some of
Ezra's Scouts had never been twenty-five miles from
home, so after winning the stake competition, it was a
great adventure for them to be transported to Logan,
Utah, for the final competition.

Anxiety and excitement mounted ever higher as the
singing Scouts from Whitney, Idaho, arrived at the
Logan Tabernacle. There they drew lots to determine the
order of appearance of the various wards. *Last!* He
laughs, recalling how he tried to crouch between the
benches to offer the boys some kind of leadership when
their turn to sing finally came. He had arranged for a

woman to play "Stars and Stripes Forever" while the boys marched into place. It was a rousing entrance that carried over into their singing. The spirited rendition won them first prize.

They went home literally walking on air. Through their singing Scouts, the little Whitney community of fifty families had come out top winner in the whole area. Ezra had promised the Scouts that if they won first place he would take them on a special hike. "A promise made is a debt unpaid," to Ezra Taft Benson, so at the next Scout meeting they made their plans to hike over the mountains to Bear Lake, thirty miles away in another valley. It was a very businesslike meeting. A group of winners was claiming their reward, and all things had to be considered very carefully. At one point a twelve-year-old Scout raised his hand and formally addressed the popular Scoutmaster.

"Mr. Scoutmaster, I'd like to make a motion."

"All right, what is it?"

"So that we will not be bothered with combs and brushes on this trip, I'd like to make a motion that we clip all our hair off."

Three or four of the older boys started to squirm in their seats. They had reached that critical age in life when they were beginning to notice girls, and short hair, they knew, would be no asset. Ezra put the question to a vote, and it carried, with the three or four older boys dissenting. Then it was stated that if these older ones didn't submit willingly they should understand that there were other ways of enforcing the rules of the troop. They submitted! Then, true to form, never missing an opportunity, one of them said, "How about the Scoutmasters?"

"It was our turn to squirm," says President Benson. But the following Saturday at the county seat, two

Scoutmasters each took a turn in the barber's chair, while the barber gleefully went over each head with the clippers. As the barber neared the end of Ezra's haircut, he said to the leaders, "If you'll let me shave your heads, I'll cut each boy's hair for nothing." And that is the way things turned out. Money was money. The hike was accomplished by twenty-four boys with heads clipped and two Scoutmasters with heads shaven.

From being a Scoutmaster with a shaved head to becoming a member of the National Advisory Council of Boy Scouts of America, Scouter Benson loved it all. He found daily reward in working with the young men themselves and over the years has been a familiar and beloved patriotic figure at national jamborees.

The stories are numerous of the blessings he has given, the warm talks he's shared with homesick Scouts, the problems he has helped solve for hundreds of young Scouts who sought the "big man in the Scouter's uniform" who would make everything all right.

For his enthusiastic support of Scouting and unique contribution, Ezra Taft Benson has been honored with the three top national awards the organization bestows—the Silver Beaver, the Silver Antelope, and the Silver Buffalo—as well as the Bronze Wolf, world Scouting's highest honor, awarded him during the general priesthood session of April 1989 conference. And at every opportunity he has delivered his fearless message to the boys and their leaders that God lives, that this country is God's promised land, and that service to others should be prepared for and performed.

One unusually large group sat fully attentive for nearly an hour while this great Scouter charged them to grow up prepared to contribute to their country. He cited examples of progress made through the efforts of young people in farm history. He told of a young man who, during World War II, learned how to make a rubber substitute from soybean oil. He told of another young researcher who developed a method to eliminate troublesome nightshade berries from the process of canning peas, a discovery which proved extremely helpful to growers. Another young person, he related, worked out a new method of converting starch in wheat to fermentable sugars.

Then Scouter Benson told about a young scientist who read about tests on phenothiazine, which was proving only moderately effective as an insecticide. This young man got the idea of trying it out on internal parasites, and the result was a new and very effective method of ridding farm animals of a whole multitude of internal parasites. Said President Benson: "I hold up these examples—there are many others—as a challenge to American youth. Take courage. Take heart. Be not afraid to dream great dreams. For truly the future of our nation depends upon the character, the self-reliance, the sense of responsibility, the skill, and the daring of our youth."

And he taught the youth to pray. Often he would pray with them as he had learned to do at the side of his father and family members, as he had done with his missionary companions and his brethren of the General Authorities. Thus it wasn't surprising that when he was secretary of agriculture he was one to suggest that cabinet meetings be opened with prayer and that President Eisenhower asked the new secretary of agriculture at the first cabinet meeting to give a prayer before the members began the business of the day. After that, it became the tradition, and during the eight years of the Eisenhower administration it was carried out—prayer before cabinet meetings.

That first prayer was reported in the press. But when Secretary Benson gave the prayer, it startled his companions in the cabinet that he used no notes, that such a magnificent prayer could be given by one who had no prior warning, no time to prepare. Mormon prayers come from the heart, and this new secretary of agriculture clearly was a man of heart, as well as one whose credentials and commitments were impressive for the job he had been given. This is that patriot's prayer as he reconstructed it for the press, who wanted a copy:

"Our Heavenly and Eternal Father, in deep humility and gratitude we approach thy holy throne in prayer. We thank thee for this blessed privilege for we realize, in part at least, our great dependence upon thee.

"We are deeply grateful for this glorious land in which we live. We know it is a land choice above all others—the greatest nation under heaven. We thank thee for all of our spiritual and material blessings. We thank thee for liberty—for our free agency, our way of life, and our free institutions.

"We acknowledge, gratefully, the unselfish service of those who have preceded us, especially the founding fathers of this nation. We thank thee for the glorious Constitution of this land, which has been established by noble men whom thou didst raise up unto this very purpose. We praise thy holy name for the glorious and eternal concepts embodied therein. Help us ever, we pray thee, to be true and faithful to these great and guiding principles.

"Our Heavenly Father, bless richly, we pray thee, thy son and servant who has been chosen by the sovereign people of this great nation, to serve as their chief executive. Our Father, wilt thou endow him, and all of us, with a deep spirit of humility and devotion. We know that without thy divine help we cannot succeed in the great responsibilities which have been placed upon us. Sustain us, our Father, through thy divine power.

"Bless in a special manner thy servant, our leader, with wisdom, understanding, and the inspiration of thy Spirit to guide him in his heavy and all-important duties. Bless him with unbounded energy, health, and strength. And may he always be blessed with wisdom and a constant spirit of discernment in his leadership.

"Bless those of us whom he has chosen to assist him and to stand at his side. May we ever uphold his hand and be true to him and to the sacred trust imposed in us. Wilt thou also bless abundantly the Congress and the judiciary. May there always be a spirit of unity in the three great branches of our government. . . .

"Guide and direct us as we go forward in our new and heavy responsibilities. Bless us with a spirit of humility. May we ever be united in seeking to know thy will and to promote the welfare of the people of this land and of the world.

"We thank thee for thy manifold blessings both material and spiritual. For this food of which we are about to partake—a further evidence and reminder of thy goodness and mercy—we thank thee. Bless and sanctify it to our nourishment and good. May we use the energy and strength derived therefrom in helping to achieve thy holy purposes.

"We ascribe unto thee the praise, the honor, and the glory for all we have achieved or may accomplish. Gratefully we dedicate our lives unto thee and to thy service. Guide and direct us in our deliberations today and always, and help us to serve with an eye single to thy glory, we humbly pray in the worthy name of thy Son, Jesus Christ, our Savior. Even So. Amen."

This prayer is worth reading again and again, for it is an example of an appropriate outpouring to God. It reveals President Benson's witness that God does live, his compassion for those who carry awesome responsibility, his understanding of the mission of the United States, and his recognition of the need for God's will to be done. Needless to say, it was a memorable and touching moment, particularly for the new president of the United States, Dwight D. Eisenhower.

"E.T.B.," as Ezra Taft Benson signed interoffice memos, recorded in his journal his first impressions of the man known as "Ike," who had been a hero in World War II, had won the confidence of the Americans, and would now serve as president. He noted that the new president was a powerfully built person, a little under six feet, with a smile "fresh and warm as a sunny summer's day, a face that seemed almost to glow with health and vigor. . . . He looked younger than his pictures indicated. As vigor was his dominant quality, the lively, blue, direct eyes were his most striking feature. You knew in an instant they mirrored the inner man, that they would reveal all his quick-changing moods: interest, welcoming warmth, delight, icy rebuke, or cold anger."

Citizen Benson liked Ike immediately.

Patriot or not, Ezra had not bargained to be the scapegoat for an administration's problems. When he tackled the job of secretary of agriculture, he had the encouragement and blessing of President McKay, who had urged Elder Benson to accept the opportunity if it came in the proper spirit. Still the politics surrounding cabinet activities were disturbing. It was rough going with the press much of the time, as well. Ezra was a patriot, all right, but was accustomed to the peace of the meetings of the Quorum of the Twelve Apostles.

What happens to a warm-hearted farm boy turned Apostle turned secretary of agriculture?—what happens to that heart? What happens to a family man, and to a

man's family, when the glaring light of political publicity
is for the first time focused upon them? Flora and Ezra
Taft Benson had tried to bring their family up to be
home-loving and unpretentious. Their own togetherness
as a family who loved the gospel of Jesus Christ was far
more important to them than all the adulation from outside that sacred circle. They participated actively in
Church affairs. Ezra Taft Benson received support from
his family as they knelt together to pray for guidance
and comfort for the beleaguered secretary of agriculture.
Although this experience as a political leader had its
challenges, it was also full of remarkable adventures and
rare opportunities to mingle with great people of the
world. As for the farm program that Secretary Benson
espoused, the struggle for this principled man came
when he saw that U.S. agriculture was on the brink of
going headlong into socialistic controls—of letting the
government subsidize and regiment. The secretary
wanted to move forward with a kind of freedom and
responsibility on the part of the farmers.

Following World War II many wanted the easy way
out of farm problems rather than face the hard facts. The
Eisenhower administration had another vision. It wasn't
popular, however, to preach "no free lunch" and "as ye
sow, so shall ye reap."

Through it all, the reputation of Ezra Taft Benson
remained untarnished. There was a serious move to draft
him as a candidate for president. He did not promote it.
But whatever hat he wore, the patriot in him inevitably
came forth. Along with whatever program he was
responsible for at the time, the plea for righteous and
informed people to preserve the Constitution and the
prosperity and freedom of America was implicit in Ezra
Taft Benson's speeches. Some years ago he quoted what
patriot Patrick Henry had said on the eve of the

American Revolution as being something he himself believed in with all his heart.

Said Henry: "There is a just God who presides over the destinies of nations and who will raise up friends to fight our battles for us." In speaking of this subject, Ezra Taft Benson has said that it is part of his own faith that, unless the political institutions are founded on faith in God and belief in the existence of moral law, no people can maintain freedom. God is the one who endowed men with the "certain inalienable rights," and no government may justly limit or destroy these.

During those years while he served in President Eisenhower's cabinet, Ezra Taft Benson said: "I have great faith in America and its people. This is a choice land. If we live and work so as to enjoy the approval of a Divine Providence, we will endure as a nation!"

> America, America!
> God shed his grace on thee,
> And crown thy good
> With brotherhood
> From sea to shining sea.

It is as if Ezra Taft Benson had penned these stirring words himself, so fervently does he preach the message. He has invested a lifetime in defending and promoting the inestimable values of God, country, freedom, and the brotherhood of man. He is an American patriot whose voice has rung out from the pulpits and podiums across the world to stir his listeners, whether they be the Boy Scouts of America or Russian citizens trying to worship according to their own desires in a discouraging environment.

One thinks of Moroni, the Book of Mormon commander, who rent his coat and wrote upon it: "In memory of our God, our religion, and freedom, and our peace, our wives, and our children." Then Moroni fastened it on the end of a pole and called it the "title of liberty." The Book of Mormon account goes on to say that Moroni bowed himself to the earth and "prayed mightily unto his God for the blessings of liberty to rest upon his brethren, so long as there should a band of Christians remain to possess the land." (Alma 46:12–13.)

President Benson, too, has a restless and unselfish desire to promote righteousness among people. That is a quality of a true patriot.

A patriot is a dedicated leader who fosters deep loyalty in his children—a particular loyalty to God, family, and country.

8

The Decision Maker

Once to every man and nation comes
    the moment to decide;
In the strife of Truth with Falsehood,
    for the good or evil side;
Some great cause, God's new Messiah,
    offering each the bloom or blight,
Parts the goats upon the left hand
    and the sheep upon the right,
And the choice goes by forever 'twixt
    that darkness and that light.
                    —James Russell Lowell

The day came for the unfolding of a more significant mission promised by Heavenly Father to a chosen child through a humble patriarch.

Ezra Taft Benson was serving as a stake president for the second time. His current assignment was the Washington, D.C. Stake, and he enjoyed that service immensely. However, he had been offered a new position, with a salary that was attractive to the father of a large and talented family. If he accepted, it would mean leaving Washington, D.C., and his stake position.

He wanted to do what the Lord wanted him to do. Before he made a decision he determined that, while he was traveling through the western states on business for the farm cooperatives, he would talk the matter over with the General Authorities of the Church in Salt Lake City.

He talked with President David O. McKay, second counselor to President Heber J. Grant, and was told that President Grant wanted to talk with him. A driver took President Benson up one of Utah's several mountain canyons to the Grant family cottage.

President Benson recalls the beauty of that summer day of July 26, 1943. Being an outdoorsman who had lived too long away from the Rocky Mountains, he probably enjoyed every minute of it. He had no intimation of what would come next.

When they arrived at the charming, secluded cottage, Sister Grant told Brother Benson to go into the bedroom where President Grant was relaxing privately. He was fully dressed, relaxing on the bed, and he asked President Benson to pull his chair close to the bedside. Then President Grant took the right hand of the younger man in both of his. His eyes were full of tears.

Then President Grant said, "Brother Benson, with all my heart I congratulate you and pray God's blessings to attend you. You have been chosen as the youngest member of the Council of the Twelve Apostles."

The new Apostle would celebrate his forty-fourth birthday just a month later. He was startled. He said later that he felt his whole world cave in around him. He had been wrestling with his own future, and, meanwhile, someone else had been planning it for him. The decision had been made two weeks earlier, but the First Presidency hadn't found just the right opportunity to talk with President Benson, they said.

Harold B. Lee was already in the Council of the Twelve, and when the two met under these new circumstances it was indeed a joyful reunion. "It was a glorious moment for two old school friends," explains President Benson. "We stood in the hall and threw our arms around each other. I admit I was overcome."

Another glorious moment came in October of that same year as Elder Benson knelt before the ailing President Heber J. Grant in the Salt Lake Temple. It was a sacred moment for him as he was ordained an Apostle and given the appropriate priesthood keys. Elder Spencer W. Kimball had immediately preceded him. Now Ezra Taft Benson not only had the same name as his revered great-grandfather but also had received the same calling. Through all of his years of service, his uppermost concern has been, "Do what is best for the kingdom."

He has traveled the world over, but it has always been a particularly pleasant experience for President Benson to go back to the place of his beginnings and meet with the Saints, to encourage their growth, and to challenge them to strengthen their programs and improve their facilities for the blessings of the families in the area.

On a visit to Lewiston, Idaho, he arrived at a time when ground had just been broken for a new stake center. "I challenged them to have it ready and paid for within a year," President Benson recalls. "If they could do that, I promised to come back and dedicate it for them, God willing. Well, I was called to go to Europe for two years, so Elder Alma Sonne did it. But they made it in less than a year! These are mighty good people in my part of the world."

On May 17, 1984, during the centennial commemoration service for the Logan Temple, President Benson gave a talk filled with references to family and neighborly influences. "I am grateful to the Lord," he said, "that my temple memories extend back—even to young boyhood." He could remember, he said, hearing his mother singing, "Have I done any good in the world today; have I helped any one in need. . . ." He also remembered his mother carefully laundering and pressing special temple clothing and explaining the sacred nature of temple work as he questioned her. "I can still see her, in my mind's eye, bending over the ironing board, with newspapers on the floor," he reminisced, "ironing long strips of white cloth, with beads of perspiration on her forehead."

President Benson grew up loving the temple because his parents loved it, and over the many years—even while President of the Church—he and Sister Benson have made visits almost every week for a temple session. He explained that he has frequently gone to the house of the Lord with a problem and with a prayer in his heart for answers. "These answers have come in clear and un-mistakable ways," he stated. (*Ensign*, August 1985, p. 8.)

"All through my life the counsel to depend on prayer has been prized above any other advice I have ever received," President Benson once said. "It has become an integral part of me, an anchor, a constant source of strength. Resorting to prayer in time of crisis was not born of desperation. It was merely the outgrowth of the cherished custom of family prayer with which I had been surrounded since earliest childhood."

President Benson paid tribute to his ancestors for teaching him that, if we will do our part and live in accordance with the divine teachings, God will not fail us—our efforts will be blessed and righteous ambitions will prosper.

On one occasion of celebration, President Benson was addressing his beloved friends in Cache Valley, and he said: "Often I have reflected upon the life and example of my great-grandfather, whose name I bear. It was said of this great exemplar of faith, freedom, and industry that the motivating force of his life was his love of God! How fortunate we would be if that same tribute could be paid each of us. Just two years before his passing he said: 'Show me an individual who lives without prayer, and I will show you an individual who lives without the bread of life. Nothing short of the bread of life that comes down from God out of heaven can supply the wants and satisfy the feelings of the Latter-day Saints and those who love truth. . . . If you suffer the Spirit of the Lord to leave your hearts and the devil comes along and finds an empty house, he enters in. . . . Of all the qualifications given me, I want most to have a testimony of Jesus Christ that will pierce like a cannonball.' "

When that pioneer Apostle's great-grandson, Ezra Taft Benson, was called to the Council of the Twelve, he reflected that same strength and witness. President Benson spoke of the glorious privilege to be blessed with wonderful opportunities for growth. "They extend back to my boyhood days in my little country ward in southern Idaho, mingling with the Saints there; and then in the mission field, back to Franklin, and then on into the Boise Stake in Idaho; then for a year in central California; and then to Washington, D.C. My greatest joy and great happiness have been those hours mingling with the Saints and with the priesthood of God. . . . I know something of the honors which men can bestow, but I know that there is nothing that can compare with the honors which come to us as servants of the Lord through the priesthood. . . . I know that God lives. This is His work. He has again spoken from the heavens with a message for the entire world; not for a handful of Latter-day Saints only, but for all our brothers and sisters, both in and out of the Church. May God give us strength to carry that message."

9

The Gifts

Yea, to be a seer, a revelator, a translator, and a
prophet, having all the gifts of God which he
bestows upon the head of the Church.
                                              —D&C 107:92

Ezra Taft Benson can read a landscape like an open
book. He was trained to do so as a boy, as a student, as
an agricultural expert. And he comes by it naturally,
being born a boy of the land, a farm boy.

He can look beyond the mosaic of fence posts, furrows, timid shoots of spring, the private cluster of outbuildings—sturdy or sagging—and fix on the owner.

He can finger the pod or the shaft, take eye of a steer, and quickly assess quality level. He can scan the color of sunset, the mist rising from the ground, the hang of the clouds over the hills, the stillness of leaves, and sense tomorrow.

It's the farmer in him.

He can hold a man's hand in a firm grip and sense that person's spiritual level. He can look a woman straight in the eye and discern her soul, intuit her need. He can gaze upon the pitiful, the confused, the sinner, and be overcome with compassion and an urgency to help.

That's the prophet in him.

When a man is a farmer, he learns things through hands-on experience. A certain kind of knowledge comes through praying over a heifer or harvesting a crop against the threat of a hailstorm. If he's had formal schooling in the matter, all the better. So it is with a prophet. From hands-on experience to leadership training and skill studies in the halls of higher learning, a man who is prepared for the task of being a spiritual guide can be more effective. President Benson is such a prophet.

Ezra Taft Benson has the heart of the farmer and the head of a leader tuned to the mind and will of God. The heart of the boy and the honor of the man have proven a winning combination for his role as prophet and President of The Church of Jesus Christ of Latter-day Saints.

President Benson is tender when he speaks of sacred experiences involving the laying on of hands—times when a humble man feels the power of God acting through him, or times when he himself is the recipient of such a blessing. The story of his own birth is a witness to the blessings that can come through the laying on of hands.

Over and over again the family rehearses the events of that date, August 4, 1899. It is a tradition of President Benson's birthday celebration that gratitude be given to God for a life spared through the power of God and the faith of his servants.

Ezra was born in a two-room cabin in a remote farm area. Medical help, equipment, training, and experience were limited. There were life-threatening complications. The country doctor told George T. Benson, Jr., that he believed he could save Sarah but that there was no hope for the child. He put the unbreathing baby aside and quickly went to work on the mother. But the grand-mothers went to work on the baby.

Each grandmother took a basin of water, one cold and one warm. The nearly twelve-pound baby was dipped alternately into one basin and then the other in an effort to shock the infant's little system into life. It worked! The baby finally uttered his first cry. Both mother and child were saved. Both flourished through ensuing years. The promises made through the laying on of hands and through prenatal blessings received in the temple were ratified.

Says President Benson, "I am grateful to my grandmothers for their swift and prayer-guided action. In a very real way, I owe them my chance to live life."

When the time came for the naming of this precious child, though other names were considered, the parents agreed that indeed he should be the namesake of the noble forebear Ezra Taft Benson, colonizer and Apostle.

Ezra was taught well from infancy. His mother made certain that he was trained in social graces as well as spiritual truths, in practical skills as well as discipline of the mind. Ezra Taft was quick to learn, and this ability, coupled with a natural sense of humor, led to happy overtones in his life. On one occasion when he was a toddler, seated in a high chair, with aunts and uncles gathered around the table at Grandmother's home, he looked over a big bowl of boiled eggs and said very courteously, "How do you do, eggs?" And he has been teased about it ever since.

The birth of each of his own children—Reed, Mark, Barbara, Beverly, Bonnie, and Flora Beth—was considered a most sacred time to Ezra Taft Benson. He has had what he calls the precious privilege of giving each of them a name and a father's blessing, of ordaining the boys to the offices of the priesthood, and of performing the wedding ceremonies in the temple for all of the children and an increasing number of grandchildren.

He has given his wife, Flora, and his family members blessings by the laying on of hands, blessings that have brought healing in times of sickness. He is grateful for this ordinance provided by God for the benefit of his spirit children. President Benson speaks warmly of the blessing given one of his daughters when she was stricken ill and he was out of the country on a Church assignment, traveling in Europe following World War II. Communication with home was very difficult. Elder Harold B. Lee was called in to give a blessing to baby Beth. The miracle happened. The crisis passed. Beth lived and grew to become a mother herself and one who relies in time of need upon this sacred priesthood ordinance of the laying on of hands.

Some years after this event the family was separated again by the call of duty to father Ezra Taft Benson. He was serving as secretary of agriculture in Washington, D.C. His family, readying their affairs so they could join him, were still in Salt Lake.

One day during this time a family friend and physician, Dr. U. R. Bryner, called Secretary Benson in Washington and told him that there had been an accident. The Benson convertible had been demolished in a collision. Daughter Barbara had suffered broken bones; Sister Benson had been more seriously hurt and hadn't regained consciousness. Instructions were given for son Reed and the bishop to administer to her. Meanwhile, Ezra cried out his own pleas. As part of the fasting and praying, the silent waiting through the night and the day full of vital government business, the secretary/husband counted, over and over again, the blessings he had received through Flora. He rehearsed the fulness she gave to his life, his need of her as he tried to fill all of his assignments.

Then the report came at last. Flora would live. After a period of recovery she would be all right. Again there was fasting and praying, this time in rejoicing over prayers that had been answered.

Many stories attest to times when President Benson has been an instrument in the hands of the Lord on behalf of others who have sought his help. One young woman who came to him had been married several years, and there had been no child born to her and her husband. Her mother had set up an appointment with President Benson for a special blessing. There had been fasting, personal prayer, and repentance—along with visits to the temple—in anticipation of this meeting with President Benson, which was to take place at 9:15 A.M., May 31, 1978. President Benson asked the young woman's father and her husband to join him in the priesthood circle. He asked the mother to kneel beside her daughter. It was a gentle and moving occasion when the power of God filled the room, not like thunder, but in a quiet, confirming swell. The words poured forth from the mouth of a prepared servant of God and were carried on the wings of the Spirit to the hearts of those present. She was blessed as a descendant of noble heritage, also a descendant of that first Ezra T. Benson. This was a heritage that would indeed be passed on to her own posterity. Then, after a long pause, a unique promise was made: she would have this posterity, but first it would be required of her to nurture spirits who would be born through different channels. They would be hers to mother first.

A few days later this family adopted a little girl. The circumstances were remarkable. When the child's birth certificate was checked, it was noted that she was born at the same moment the adoptive mother was receiving a blessing by the laying on of hands through President Benson—9:15 A.M., May 31, 1978.

There is an incident from the life of his namesake and revered great-grandfather, Ezra T. Benson, that President Benson holds sacred as an example of how the Holy Ghost can prompt and direct a needful, righteous person.

Brigham Young had sent several of the brethren to the Hawaiian Islands. Part of the journey was made by small seacraft. One day the surf was unusually high. Suddenly a fierce wave overpowered the boat and sent its passengers into the turbulent ocean. Along with some other passengers, the missionaries—Elder Ezra T. Benson, Elder Alma Smith, and Elder W. W. Cluff— managed to swim to the boat and catch hold. Elder Lorenzo Snow, who was traveling with them, was thrown out of the boat, too, but he did not surface for some time. Native divers searched the waters again and again for him. At last someone noticed Elder Snow's white hair floating on the water. He was quickly rescued and brought to shore.

There seemed to be no life in Elder Snow as they rolled him over one of the empty barrels stored on the beach. They worked frantically, trying to force out the water he had swallowed. They placed their hands upon his head and gave him a powerful blessing. They cried out to God in their hearts, as each took a turn working against Elder Snow's rib cage to revive him. What to do?

Then, responding to a flash of inspiration, they blew in through Elder Snow's mouth, trying to inflate the lungs again. The group took turns and continued to work in this manner on the stricken man, without let up, until finally he breathed on his own. This is a remarkable incident for many reasons, but it is particularly interesting when one remembers that it is only in comparatively recent years that mouth-to-mouth resuscitation has been standard revival procedure.

This is one of the Benson family's treasured stories that they teach their children in order to reinforce principles such as the power of prayer and the workings of the Holy Ghost. George counseled his son Ezra from the boy's childhood that this story was proof that he was never alone. Heavenly Father is always near and ready to help if a person will turn to him in humble prayer and seek his will.

There is another incident from the life of young Ezra that has stayed with the man all of his life. It is an example of the working of God in the life of a devoted person who claims the blessings of being baptized and confirmed and having the Holy Ghost bestowed upon him. Ezra and his cousin George were born about the same time in the same community. They were fast friends, too. As young men they joined the army as part of the World War I forces and were assigned to what today would be called the Reserve Officers' Training Corps (ROTC) at the college in Logan.

They were given two weeks furlough to go home and help harvest the beets. They had planned to leave ROTC camp for home on Saturday. Friday morning Ezra woke up with a strong impression that he should go home that day instead of waiting until Saturday. He left, but his cousin George stayed. That day the killer flu epidemic of that period broke out in ROTC camp. George, who slept in a cot on one side of young Ezra, and the man who slept on the other side both died. President Benson became ill, too, but he was home, where he received a powerful priesthood blessing of healing at the hands of his father and loving, tender nursing care from his mother. President Benson has always felt that had he stayed back at camp with George, no doubt he would have died like the others.

During this time a favorite aunt named Louise, who took a keen interest in Ezra and who also served on a general board of the Church, under inspiration promised him that one of his great-grandfather's descendants would have a high-ranking place in the Church. President Benson never forgot the feeling that filled him as his aunt made that remark, though he did not personalize it at the time. There was not the slightest inkling in his own mind that he was the descendant referred to; rather, he thought he had been spared to help prepare one of his relatives, perhaps.

Spiritual experiences have always been part of Ezra Taft Benson's life, and he has accepted them within the sacred context of gifts from God. He counts such blessings as part of his lifelong preparation to serve as President of the Church and as prophet to a growing multitude of Saints, educated and discriminating members, humble seekers after truth.

His preparation began early. Impressions are still clear in his mind about the positive feelings his parents had toward the Church and its leadership. Example can be a stronger teacher than lectures or discipline. Attitudes filter from the parent to the proverbial twig that is being bent at their hands.

His parents' devotion is indicative of the strong attitude with which the prophet Ezra Taft Benson counsels the Saints on family life and parenting. By following his example of obedience and striving, all fathers—indeed all people—can become heirs to the sacred gifts of the Spirit which God has promised His faithful children. And that makes all the difference in a life.

10

A Man of the Lord

And if thou art faithful unto the end thou shalt have
a crown of immortality, and eternal life in the
mansions which I have prepared in the house of my
Father.

—D&C 81:6

Following April 1978 conference my brother Judge
Aldon J. Anderson and I were invited to take a very
sentimental journey with President and Sister Benson
back to the President's "fatherland" near Whitney,

Idaho. It was a journey back to their beginnings to renew the understanding of "from whence we had come."

As we were leaving Salt Lake, President Benson asked Aldon to stop the car for a moment. Then he turned to me and invited me to ask Heavenly Father to bless us in a special way as we made this tender pilgrimage. One understands the present better in terms of the past. Armed with such understanding the hope of the future is increased twofold, according to President Benson's thoughts at that time.

We had visited the farm area in Whitney, the academy in Preston, and now we were driving along a country road heading for the Whitney town cemetery. This adventure into the past just wouldn't be complete without a visit to the grave sites of loved ones.

As the Bensons pointed out this headstone here and that marker there, with some remembrance shared of the person whose particular grave it was, President Benson confessed: "I have met so many interesting and famous people in my life, but there isn't one of them better than the people from Whitney, Idaho. These people buried here are the people who influenced my early life by their lives, their principles, their sacrifice, their goodness.

"At Ernest Wilkinson's funeral, I quoted something that I believe in deeply," he continued. "The Prophet Joseph, talking at a funeral, emphasized the resurrection by telling about the vision he had of it. The vision was of people who were holding out their hands to greet another person rising from the grave. He noted what a joy it would be in the morning of the resurrection if we had been laid close to our father, our mother, our brother, our sister, our spouse, and our children."

Then President Benson patted Sister Benson's arm, which was hooked through his. "We feel this," he said, "and so Flora and I have obtained a family plot in the Whitney cemetery."

We walked across the hard sod of spring to a place near the northwest corner of the cemetery. This special plot was protected by tall blue spruce. A marker of polished granite had been etched with the names of Ezra Taft and Flora Amussen Benson. On the opposite side was the inscription: "Children born of this eternal unit: Reed Amussen, Mark Amussen, Barbara Amussen, Beverly Amussen, Bonnie Amussen, and Flora Beth."

Flora Amussen Benson, devoted mother, stroked her hand tenderly over the names of her children.

We stood silent for a moment in the quiet, breathing the clean country air of that place they love. This faithful couple, so very much alive, surveyed their burial site in an attitude of comfort and peace.

"It is a heavenly spot," she said.

"Yes," I responded. "Peaceful. Sacred, almost." I turned to President Benson and said, "But you can't be buried way up here in Idaho. It is too far from Salt Lake."

"Oh, Flora and I will be buried here, all right. At the time we bought this plot I asked President McKay and he gave his permission."

"But it's such a distance from the headquarters of the Church," I persisted, "and you will be the prophet some day."

One day circumstances arose, and the time of ripening was done. Ezra Taft Benson became the mouthpiece of God on earth—a man of the Lord and a spiritual father to a great selection of God's children gathering in increasing numbers across the world.

Among the first public words that people heard from their new leader were these: "My heart has been filled with an overwhelming love and compassion for all members of the Church and our Heavenly Father's children everywhere. I love all our Father's children of every color, creed, and political persuasion." (*Ensign*, December 1985, p. 5.)

A loving prophet.

Like an understanding father.

People could be farmers or not, from Whitney or not, business people, educators, struggling nonbelievers, victims in war-torn countries, and this great-hearted man felt love toward them all. Such is his gift from God.

A humble prophet, more than a prepared, powerful executive—a high-principled leader, a loving man.

This love is reflected in a First Presidency message entitled "An Invitation to Come Back." Addressed primarily to less active and estranged Church members, it reads in part:

"We are aware of some who are less active, of others who have become critical and are prone to find fault, and of those who have been disfellowshipped or excommunicated because of serious transgressions.

"To all such we reach out in love. The Lord said, 'I, the Lord, will forgive whom I will forgive, but of you it is required to forgive all men' (D&C 64:10).

"We encourage members to forgive those who may have wronged them. To those who have ceased activity and to those who have become critical, we say, 'Come back. Come back and feast at the table of the Lord, and taste again the sweet and satisfying fruits of fellowship with the saints.'

"We are confident that many have longed to return, but have felt awkward about doing so. We assure you that you will find open arms to receive you and willing hands to assist you."

A compassionate prophet. A caring father.

This great and loving leader has also tirelessly and fervently encouraged people in the study of the Book of Mormon. His emphasis on this additional witness for Christ reflects his own diligence as a student of the word of God.

Ezra Taft Benson—a disciple of Christ, a student of the word.

Since his beginnings on the farm in Idaho, life has helped polish Ezra Taft Benson for such a time as this. The people, the places, and the opportunities in his life prepared him. His study of the Book of Mormon and other scriptures containing the revealed word of God has helped him make wise choices. He has sought wise counsel. He has learned devotion to duty and the characteristic Benson exactness in performance. He values the worth of souls and is forever committed to helping people become more righteous. He has been touched by the Spirit of God and marked by circumstance and ordination to be a prophet, a spiritual leader to the Saints.

This leader and father has faithfully followed after his fathers and moved ever closer to Heavenly Father and the Lord Jesus Christ as he has carried forth their errand. With Ezra Taft Benson—a boy of the land and a man of the Lord—the people feel secure, confident, directed by a certain trumpet. Everything will be all right.